Worship Planning
Resources for
Every Sunday of the Year

The Abingdon
Worship Annual

2023

Edited by

Mary Scifres
and B. J. Beu

Abingdon Press / Nashville

THE ABINGDON WORSHIP ANNUAL 2023:
WORSHIP PLANNING RESOURCES
FOR EVERY SUNDAY OF THE YEAR

Copyright © 2022 by Abingdon Press

ISBN 978-1-7910-2381-2

All lectionary verses and all Scripture quotations, unless noted otherwise, are taken from the Common English Bible (CEB), copyright 2011. Used by permission. All rights reserved.

MANUFACTURED IN THE UNITED STATES OF AMERICA

Contents

CONTENTS

October

November

December

Introduction

Planning Virtual Worship–
Pandemic or Not!

Until the global pandemic of 2020, very few of our readers had been planning worship for the virtual world. Some livestreamed or recorded worship services for homebound members, but very few put much thought into those virtual options in their creative thinking and planning. Now, almost all of us do. With that in mind, B. J. and I offer some insights and ideas to you, gleaned from your colleagues around the world.

Adapting Liturgy for Online Worship

Contained in these pages, you will find carefully and caringly crafted prayers and readings, along with theme ideas and centering words to help you and your congregation focus each week as you worship together. When worshiping online, we have all learned that some of our former traditions don't work as well in the virtual world. For responsive readings, inviting two leaders to read back and forth rather than one reader awaiting a congregation's unison response can be much more effective in livestream or video conference worship gatherings. Similarly, unison readings and singing are not that effective online due to the different timing. Instead, we encourage single readers—preferably various laypeople throughout the church year—to lead those formerly "unison" moments while others are encouraged to read along quietly, silently, or aloud with one another in their homes (while being "muted" online). If live streaming, intentionally add a moment of pause before and after any unison "in person" moments for the time delay that live streamers often experience as they worship from other locations. The moment of pause helps unify both congregations, while also allowing the gentle breath of the Holy Spirit to breathe a pause into our worshiping rhythm. Feel free to share the prayers and readings from within these pages not only online, but even in weekly e-newsletters or devotionals. Note the copyright and authorship, and then share with your people in creative ways to nourish their spiritual journeys. Let us know if you have questions about ways to innovate your use of liturgy and worship words, as we want to support and strengthen your ministry and that of your congregations.

Versions of Virtual Worship

There are many ways of worshiping together, whether worshiping in our homes, outdoors, in church buildings, or some combination thereof. For years, homebound and traveling church members have yearned to stay connected with their church families. Now, almost all of us have developed methods for staying connected through our computers, tablets, and phones. We hope you will continue connecting in these virtual ways, even when the dangers of a pandemic have passed. The more we can connect without regard to geography, the more inclusive our worship services and congregational relationships can be. Imagine how much joy we bring our homebound "visitors" when they stream worship right into their living rooms and assisted-living apartments. To stay "connected" in the past, my homebound grandmother had to rely on copies of *The Upper Room* and visits from her pastor. Now, all who can't attend Sunday worship can stay connected with your congregation, thanks to modern technology and the church's amazing willingness and ability to adapt in 2023!

As the pandemic spread around our globe, we watched colleagues without the ability to live stream create amazing possibilities from their smartphones, camcorders, and tablets. The following methods categorize some of the ways you have made virtual worship possible for your people.

1. Pre-recorded worship filmed in "one take"—weekly sermons, musical offerings, or even midweek devotions.

2. Pre-recorded worship filmed separately in various segments from multiple leaders and locations—distributed as individual elements or edited into a complete recorded worship service.

3. Pre-recorded musical offerings filmed from multiple participants and locations—edited into a virtual choir or ensemble.

4. Livestreamed sermons, meditations, or devotions.

5. Livestreamed worship services, inclusive of sermon, music, and liturgy.

6. Video-conference worship, using a service like Zoom, to allow for interaction and fellowship in the worship experience.

We applaud you for creating such beautiful worship in so many innovative ways! Below, we take a closer look at each of the methods noted above.

Pre-recorded worship, weekly sermons, and musical offerings that are filmed in "one take" can be done with a simple smartphone, computer, or basic recording camera. For best results recording with a phone or camera, purchase a simple tripod or stand to provide stability for the camera and allow the leader to focus on the words or music you are offering. The "one-take" option, while not as polished as edited versions, allows for both simplicity and authenticity. Be honest with your congregation that this recording is essentially "live," even though it's pre-recorded. Be honest with yourself that the "one-take" option leaves you more vulnerable as a leader than edited versions. This option frees up an enormous amount of time and cost over methods requiring extensive editing, so that worship isn't the only ministry you have the time or money to provide in a given week. For distribution and communication ideas, see the next paragraph.

Pre-recorded worship filmed in various segments from multiple leaders and locations that are distributed as individual elements allows diverse and varied worship moments to be shared with your fellowship throughout the week, rather than as a single service. One pastor walked his deserted streets the first week communities were sheltering at home as his videographer recorded him with a drone video camera. The voice-over (added later) was both haunting and comforting as the pastor shared both his concerns and his hopes for his congregation and our world. Another pastor recorded all of her summer sermons from her dock, with a beautiful lake in the background, taking her congregation through a series of "lakeshore" stories of Jesus and the disciples. In both cases, their churches also distributed links to instrumental and vocal music from their church musicians. One church included weekly links to children's messages from volunteers in their Christian education program. When individuals use their own equipment to record these segments, the quality can vary widely. Some churches address this issue by having participants visit the sanctuary at scheduled times so that a videographer can record each segment, or they advise participants in use of common equipment and methods. For example, one church asks each volunteer who records a prayer or song to record it horizontally on a smartphone, using the phone's built-in microphone. Some church administrators and pastors share the links to the various recordings on the church website or in emails with PDF documents. Others post each segment on their social media channels as the segment is created, which allows for spiritual nurture throughout the week. Others wait and send all of the links in a weekly post to create a more unified feel to worship, even when it is created in different segments. Consider sharing prayers and readings from this resource with a variety of volunteer and staff worship leaders throughout your worship year, to expand both participation and creativity in the worship experience. Remind them they are permitted to adapt, edit, or use the resources exactly as they are written in both written and recorded format. Just note the authorship and copyright notice in whatever written communication accompanies your recordings.

Pre-recorded worship filmed in various segments from multiple leaders and locations edited into one worship

service provides a fuller and more familiar worship experience for congregants. As with the previous style, recording from various locations provides a great deal of creativity and variety, but varying sound levels and quality of recordings can present a challenge for your video editor. Most churches find that the editing is simplified if all recordings are shot in one location using the same equipment, with leaders scheduled at various times to provide for safe physical distancing. This option requires more preparation and planning, along with a paid editor or very generous volunteer who can handle the demands of post-production editing. Our son, Michael Beu, a video editor, works with a number of churches and pastors to manage the technical and time-consuming demands of editing and posting their worship videos, or helps them find volunteers or train staff members to do so. This extra help allows pastors to focus on worship rather than on technology, and many church donors have stepped up to provide the financial support necessary for this new way of providing worship and spiritual nurture.

For the worship experience, some churches "premiere" worship services put together in this way by scheduling the uploaded video to go "live" at a specific time on their social media channel. This allows and encourages congregants to watch and worship "together" at the same time from their various locations and also can provide viewers the opportunity for interactive chat on the social media channel, creating a sense of community. This sense of community is increased if the worship service is followed by a virtual fellowship time via video conferencing on platforms like Zoom or Skype. Others "open" the posted worship service video immediately, once editing and uploading is complete, so that worshipers can view and worship whenever they want. One of our readers prefers this latter option, so that her church can join for virtual fellowship and sermon conversation during the normal Sunday morning worship time, having viewed worship the day before.

Pre-recorded musical offerings filmed from multiple participants and locations that are edited into a virtual choir or ensemble allow vocal music and ensemble music to be a part of our lives even when it is unsafe to "make music" in the same space or when we want to create ensembles with people who live in different parts of the globe. Solo offerings are, of course, more easily achieved even with simple recording devices—sometimes connected directly to an electronic musical instrument, other times recorded with the internal microphone provided on the recording device. Most musicians prefer the higher quality of recording with an external microphone, attached to the video-recording device. Virtual ensembles require a great deal of post-production sound editing. It's harder than it looks and sounds, and yet many brave musicians and film editors have taken on the task and learned the necessary technology to bring these virtual ensembles to their congregations.

Livestreamed sermons, meditations, or devotionals are being offered by churches at all times of day and night around our globe. They can be recorded and offered on almost any social media channel by clicking on their livestream option. One colleague records a daily devotional video, but also posts it in written format on his Facebook page. (He also enlists church leaders to record on Fridays and Saturdays, so he can enjoy sabbath and family time on those days.) Consider using prayers and responsive readings from this resource to enhance devotionals, sermons, or reflective meditations you are providing for your people.

Livestreamed worship services that include sermons, music, and liturgy require recording equipment connected to a livestreaming service and, ideally, a wired connection to the internet. Most churches who choose this option have invested considerable money into a streaming broadcast system and budget for trained staff members who know how to operate both the recording and broadcasting systems. As with the virtual choir option, this isn't as easy as it looks! But it is a beautiful option for churches that have the ability and the resources. That said, most churches who were streaming before the pandemic have both adapted and improved their livestream worship ministry. Before the pandemic, much of livestreamed worship was either an afterthought of what was already happening on Sundays or a polished "performance." Now, some of the fanciest live streams have become the simplest. There is an elegance to this simplicity and this intentionality, when worship is crafted to focus on one primary theme or message. Worship services have been shortened to adapt to the shorter attention span of a virtual congregation. Messages and musical offerings are less polished and more personal, creating intimacy and relationship with viewers at home. Don't be fooled, though! The technology in the background to make livestreaming successful is complex with little room for error, which occurs frequently for a variety of reasons. Those of us who livestream on a regular basis have learned to laugh at ourselves, forgive technology, and patiently await our technicians to address the glitches that inevitably arise. One colleague laughingly posted on our clergy Facebook group, "It's time to designate a 'Glitch Sunday!'"

Video-conference worship, using providers like Zoom, provides opportunities for interaction and fellowship during the worship experience. While this format creates a more collaborative environment, it requires more flexibility and informality for both leaders and participants. Best practice for this format has participants and members log onto the video conference *with a private church link* in order to prevent interruptions by internet trolls. Designate a video-conference coordinator to welcome guests, help with password and technology challenges, monitor chat questions or comments, and mute everyone but the participants once worship begins. A video-conference coordinator allows pastors, musicians, and worship leaders to focus on their worship responsibilities without having to control the service's complicated technical requirements.

When the pastor and designated leaders are leading, their video feeds should be the only ones with active microphones. This allows people to hear more clearly and participate more fully without interrupting the worship flow. While microphones are muted, congregational singing, unison and responsive readings, and responses to the Spirit are all possible in this format. If you have a solo worship leader, make sure their microphone is always unmuted so that they can lead the singing, readings, and prayers. To add an interactive component, encourage people to comment in their chat box, or even invite conversation following the message by designating a time of unmuted sermon feedback and Q & A. Similarly, community prayer, and joys and concerns can be interactive by unmuting members for these worship elements; but be sure to mute the members again before praying the pastoral or the Lord's Prayer. Although you can use a webinar format instead, webinars are more "presentation" than "participation," similar to a Facebook Live or YouTube Premiere.

Choosing or Changing Your Version of Virtual Worship

Several decisions need to be made before settling on a method of virtual worship:

1. Whom is God calling your church to reach? What technology are they able and willing to access?

2. What type of worship experience will best serve the congregation you are called to reach?

3. How much is your church able and willing to spend, both in time and money?

4. What technology and distribution platform best addresses these questions?

With these decisions in mind, you are ready to work with your worship team to create a virtual worship design and choose a platform best suited to your current needs. What you started with need not limit where you go in 2023 and beyond. Similarly, if you've been doing this alone, you need not continue doing it alone. This is the perfect time to create a worship team that will work with you, supporting and strengthening both the process and creativity of your worship experience. When planned and implemented alone, virtual worship is already leading to many early retirements and departures from ministry. The workload is simply too exhausting and isolating to sustain by one individual, regardless of how talented they are. Reach out to your leadership, your colleagues, and even community partners to find the help you need. If you're reading this article but not on the worship team, check with your pastor or musician to see if they need support and help. Contact us if you need help figuring out how to find and work with a team.

Adapting Music and Liturgy for Social Distancing and Safety

One of the greatest challenges in church worship today has been the limitations placed on vocal music and the spoken word to avoid spreading infection. Yet, limitations give rise to creativity and new ways for musicians to stay involved in ministry. Some vocal choirs have transitioned into bell choirs. Other vocalists have been reading the texts of favorite hymns or anthems, while instrumentalists play the music underneath. Some churches are pre-recording vocal music for presentation on-screen during live worship, while simultaneously streaming the live worship and the pre-recorded music for their virtual worshipers. Responsive and unison readings are not always the safest option for a congregation gathered together, but two readers may "duet" a responsive reading from the chancel while remaining safely distanced from both worshipers and one another. Or again, music might enhance a solo voice reciting the Lord's Prayer. Looking for more creative ideas? Visit **maryscifresministries.com** to find some of the creative ways B. J. and Mary are working to address the changing forms of worship.

Adapting Virtual Worship to a Hybrid Form

Over these last few years, you have likely led worship in a variety of ways, adapting to social restrictions the pandemic has thrown our way. As churches re-open their sanctuaries, while also offering virtual worship, we have begun calling this new *both-and* situation *hybrid worship*. Our worship services are no longer just the old fossil-fueled combustion engine of sanctuary worship, but also electric-fueled worship of videos streamed directly into the homes of church members and friends around the globe. One colleague welcomed a North Carolina family into membership in his California church three thousand miles away. When their sanctuary reopened, the North Carolina family continued to participate and connect through the many online worship and study group opportunities of their California church home, growing more and more deeply connected regardless of geographical distance. As congregations again gather for in-person worship, this hybrid model allows us to continue serving our virtual worshipers. To prepare for this, worship leaders have put tech crews in place who can record the services, upload to an online platform, and communicate with the congregation how to access the online service. Your best practice is for worship leaders to focus on the worship components (music, message, liturgy) and for tech and administrative team members to focus on the technology and communication components. Let us know if you have questions or concerns we can help you address, or if you have insights and ideas to share with others.

Mary Scifres & B. J. Beu
admin@maryscifres.com

January 1, 2023

Epiphany of the Lord

Joanne Brown

[handwritten: 288 we Three Kings; 281 what Child is This]

COLOR

White

SCRIPTURE READINGS

Isaiah 60:1-6; Psalm 72:1-7, 10-14; Ephesians 3:1-12; Matthew 2:1-12 *[circled]*

THEME IDEAS

In the Northern Hemisphere, we are experiencing the darkness of midwinter. Days are short and nights long. But there are other forms of darkness—poverty, war, injustice, oppression, hatred, prejudice, fear—forms that affect us just as they did the people of biblical times. But in these passages, light breaks through the darkness: a prophet calls us to arise and see the light of liberation and peace, reconciliation and joy; the psalmist prays for a ruler who will light the way of his people with righteousness, prosperity, and an end to oppression and injustice. The writer of Ephesians lights the way through mystery, with a message of the good news of Christ Jesus; and the magi follow the light of a star, finding more than they were looking for to return home transformed.

INVITATION AND GATHERING

Centering Words (Isaiah 60)
Arise; shine, for your light has come.

Call to Worship (Isaiah 60, Matthew 2)
Arise; shine, for your light has come!
We are called out of our darkness into light.
Lift up your eyes and look around.
We rejoice in the gift of light.
Come, let us worship the God of light and joy and peace.
**We come to kneel at the cradle of the babe,
the light incarnate.**

–OR–

Call to Worship
Light shines in on the darkness of the world!
Can you see it? Can you feel it?
**We will open the eyes of our hearts
and light the light within.**
There's a star beckoning us to follow.
We will see where it leads us today in worship.
Let's see where it leads.
**We will watch as we go about our days,
our weeks, and the rest of our lives.**

Opening Prayer (Isaiah 60, Matthew 2)
God of promise and light, open our eyes this morning,
that we may see your light in the darkness.
Open our hearts,
that we may perceive your promises
of justice and righteousness—
promises fulfilled in the babe of Bethlehem.

May we, like the magi, have a star to guide us
on our journey quest to find the one
who will truly set us free.
May this time of worship bring us closer to you,
that the good news of the birth of light and love
may transform our lives. Amen.

PROCLAMATION AND RESPONSE

Prayer of Confession (Isaiah 60, Ephesians 3, Matthew 2)
Ever patient God, we are a people
who live in thick darkness.
We stumble around,
bombarded by news of war and poverty,
famine and genocide.
We easily lose our bearings.
The maelstrom of life can overwhelm and paralyze us
when we need to be at our best.
Help us be people who shine the light
of your righteousness, peace, and joy
into the dark places of our lives
and our world.
Unlock the mystery and glory
of the babe born in Bethlehem.
Guide us with your star of wonder
and turn our aimless wanderings
into journeys of purpose.

Words of Assurance
As certain as the dawn follows the night,
so is the promise of God's forgiveness and love.
Arise and shine.
Follow the star, that the light born in Bethlehem
may transform our world from darkness into light.

3

Passing the Peace of Christ (Matthew 2)

Lift your eyes and look around. The light of the babe of Bethlehem shines from the face of each one of us here. Greet this light in one another, rejoicing in being together, as we pass the peace of Christ, our joy and our hope.

Invitation to the Word

Open our hearts and minds to the light of your word, read and preached.

Response to the Word (Matthew 2)

We rejoice in the mystery
made plain through the good news
of the babe of Bethlehem.
May this good news transform us and guide us,
as we seek to follow the star of love and light.

THANKSGIVING AND COMMUNION

Invitation to the Offering (Isaiah 60, Matthew 2)

We have seen the light of the world.
We have been called to follow the star of promise.
Like the magi before us,
let us bring our gifts to honor the Christ child;
let us bring God's light to all the dark places
in our community and in our world.

Offering Prayer (Isaiah 60)

God of light and promise, we bring our gifts
to further your work in a dark world.
May they bring your light
to those who are overwhelmed
by darkness, pain, and loneliness.
Accept these gifts of money and time—
the gifts of our very selves.

May they shine for all to see
    and be brought into the sphere
        of your love and righteousness.

SENDING FORTH

Benediction (Isaiah 60, Matthew 2)
    Arise, and go forth to shine for all the world to see.
        We go to spread the good news of light and love,
        the hope of righteousness and justice.
    Follow the star that will guide you on your journey—
    this week, this year, and forevermore.
        We go forth, as the magi of old,
        transformed by the presence of the child of light.
    May the blessing of the God of light
    rest upon you and fill you with light.
        Amen.

January 8, 2023

Baptism of the Lord

B. J. Beu
Copyright © B. J. Beu

COLOR

White

[handwritten: 104 O worship the King
& Come Thou Almighty King]

SCRIPTURE READINGS

Isaiah 42:1-9; (Psalm 29) Acts 10:34-43; Matthew 3:13-17

THEME IDEAS

God's servant in whom God delights, the one blessed with the power and strength of God's Spirit, focuses our readings. Isaiah proclaims that this servant will bring justice and righteousness. Matthew proclaims that this servant is none other than the messiah, the fulfillment of Israel's hopes and dreams. On Baptism of the Lord Sunday, we remember Jesus's baptism—a baptism of both purifying water and empowering Spirit. Truly, we are a people of both water and the Spirit.

INVITATION AND GATHERING

Centering Words (Matthew 3)

Come to the waters of baptism. Touch the Spirit's power. Feel the Spirit's loving embrace. Come and be made new.

Call to Worship **(Psalm 29, Matthew 3)**
The voice of God calls over the waters:
"Beloved, receive the Holy Spirit."
The Son of God beckons:
"Beloved, be born of water and the Spirit."
The Spirit of God proclaims:
"Beloved, be born anew this day."
The voice of God calls through our baptism.
Come! Let us worship.

–OR–

Call to Worship (Isaiah 42)
Holy waters call us here.
We are a people of the water.
Splash and play in holy springs.
We are a people of the Spirit.
Wash in the fount of Christ's love.
We are a people of God's grace.
Come! Our baptism calls us here.

Opening Prayer (Isaiah 42, Psalm 29, Matthew 3)
Spirit of righteousness, God of power and might,
help us be a light to the nations
and a reflection of your glorious salvation.
Work in our lives and in our ministries,
that the world might know
the power of your love and grace.
As you alighted upon Jesus at his baptism,
descend upon us this day,
that we may be a people of hope
and possibility.
Wash us clean and renew our spirits,
through Jesus Christ, our lord. Amen.

7

PROCLAMATION AND RESPONSE

Prayer of Yearning (Acts 10, Matthew 3)
Gentle Spirit, Holy Dove,
reclaim us through the waters of our baptism.
As we long to be more than we have become,
remake us through the power of your love.
In our yearning to taste the fullness of life,
restore us through the wonder of your grace.
In our desire to live as your beloved children,
make us instruments of your kingdom building,
that we may be a light to the nations,
and a source of hope
to those who sit in darkness. Amen.

Words of Assurance (Psalm 29, Matthew 3)
Listen to the voice that calls forth creation,
claims Jesus at his baptism and speaks to us still:
"You are my beloved; receive the Holy Spirit."
Rest in this assurance and live in the Spirit.

Passing the Peace of Christ (Matthew 3)
Turn to your neighbor and behold the light of Christ
within each face you see. See one another as God's beloved children—children baptized with water and the
Spirit, children who abide in the grace of the living God.
Greet one another in spirit and in truth as you share
signs of Christ's peace.

Response to the Word (Isaiah 42, Psalm 29, Matthew 3)
God has shown us what is good and pleasing.
Christ has blessed us with new life,
through the power of the Holy Spirit.
Sing of God's glory for all to hear.
Shine Christ's light for all to see.

Live as Christ's disciples.
Love as children of the living God.

THANKSGIVING AND COMMUNION

Offering Prayer (Psalm 29, Acts 10)
Be in the gifts we bring before you, O God,
as you are ever in the gift of our baptism.
Renew your people through this offering,
as you have renewed us with your presence this day,
through Jesus Christ, our Lord. Amen.

Reaffirmation of Our Baptismal Covenant
The voice of God calls:
"Come to the healing waters and be made whole."
Make us whole, O God.
The Son of God beckons:
"Receive the fire of the Spirit and be reborn."
Renew us once more, Great Spirit.
The Spirit of God summons:
"Come into the presence of Love."

SENDING FORTH

Benediction (Psalm 29, Matthew 3)
Rejoice in the glory of your baptism
each and every day.
We will live in the power of the Holy Spirit.
Let your spirits soar like eagles
but be as gentle as doves.
We will drink deep from the waters of grace.
Go forth to announce the glory of our God.
We go, renewed and made whole,
as a blessing to all.

January 15, 2023

Second Sunday after the Epiphany

Mary Scifres
Copyright © Mary Scifres

435 Word of Grace

COLOR *16 All Hail the Power*

Green

SCRIPTURE READINGS

Isaiah 49:1-7; Psalm 40:1-11; 1 Corinthians 1:1-9; John 1:29-42

THEME IDEAS

God sees us as the miracles we are. Each of today's scriptures reveals the "bigness" that most of us deny ourselves as we reflect on who we are as God's creation and as God's followers. Isaiah understands his role to be bigger than as a prophet to Israel alone as he calls Israel to be a light to the nations. Paul reminds the Corinthians that they have every spiritual gift and total enrichment in Christ. And Jesus proclaims that Simon is no longer a mere fisherman but is the rock upon which the church will be built. We are so much more than we realize. Until we realize that we are God's precious creation, created in God's own image and called to be God's light and love in the world, we will never see ourselves as God sees us.

INVITATION AND GATHERING

Centering Words (Isaiah 49)
> Let your light shine. Be a light to your community. Be
> a light to the nations. Be a light to the whole world. Let
> your light shine.

Call to Worship (Isaiah 49, John 1)
> Called to be light,
> **we come this day to shine.**
> Called to follow Christ,
> **we come this day to serve.**
> Called to love God,
> **we come to worship and praise.**

Opening Prayer (Isaiah 49, 1 Corinthians 1)
> Light of the world, shine through our worship,
> that we might see you more clearly
> and know you more intimately.
> Reveal your presence and make your voice heard,
> that we may grow in love
> and shine with the light of your love
> for all to see. Amen.

PROCLAMATION AND RESPONSE

Prayer of Yearning (Isaiah 49, Psalm 40, 1 Corinthians 1)
> Great and mighty God,
> show us how wondrously and mysteriously
> you have created us.
> We yearn to shine as brightly for you,
> as you shine for us.
> We long to see ourselves as the amazing creations
> you intend us to be.

Inspire us with your mercy and your grace,
that we might know how deeply enriched we are
in your love.
For you have given us the spiritual gifts we need
to answer your call and live into our purpose.

Words of Assurance (1 Corinthians 1)
God's strength courses through us,
that we may be blameless
in the loving mercy of Christ.

Passing the Peace of Christ (Isaiah 49, 1 Corinthians 1)
Share light and love with those you meet and greet this
day.

Introduction to the Word (Psalm 40, Isaiah 49)
Wait patiently.
Listen openly.
Trust that God's loving light and law
will be revealed in these words and in your hearts.

Response to the Word
Light of all creation, shine through us,
that others may see your presence living in us.
Shine in our world, even in the deepest darkness,
that all people may come to know your light
and your love.
Shine through all of creation,
that the world you dream for
might come fully into being.

THANKSGIVING AND COMMUNION

Invitation to the Offering (1 Corinthians 1)
Every gift we need is already here. Let us bring our gifts, whether we deem them small or large, and trust that they are enough.

Offering Prayer (John 1, Isaiah 49)
Lamb of God, bless these gifts with your mercy
and your grace.
Shine through these gifts with your light and love,
that our ministries and our church
may be a beacon of light and love,
revealing your presence to our world.

SENDING FORTH

Benediction (John 1, Isaiah 49)
Shine brightly, for you are the light of the world.
Shine with light and love.
Shine for all to see!

January 22, 2023

Third Sunday after the Epiphany

Karin Ellis

COLOR *342 Rock of Ages*
Green *630 what a Friend*

SCRIPTURE READINGS

Isaiah 9:1-4; Psalm 27:1, 4-9; 1 Corinthians 1:10-18;
Matthew 4:12-23

THEME IDEAS

During this Season of Epiphany, we continue to see how
the light of God shines in the darkness and in our lives.
Isaiah 9 proclaims that those who walked in darkness
have seen a great light. The psalmist reminds us that we
do not have to turn away from God; we can turn toward
God's love and light. Then we will sing songs of joy. In
his letter to the Corinthians, Paul instructs the body of
Christ to refrain from fighting among themselves, but
rather proclaim the message of Christ. In Matthew's
Gospel, we hear of Jesus withdrawing to be by himself
and then calling his first disciples. Throughout these
scriptures there is a call to follow God, to seek Christ,
and to look for the light.

INVITATION AND GATHERING

Centering Words (Isaiah 9, Psalm 27)
Where there is darkness, there is also light. Look for the
light—places of love, joy, grace, and hope.

Call to Worship (Psalm 27)
We come seeking God,
the one who guides us and protects us.
People of God, there is nothing to fear,
for God dwells in our hearts.
Let us shout with joy, for God is here!
Let us sing praises to the Holy One!

Opening Prayer (Isaiah 9, Matthew 4)
God of light, we come tired and weary,
carrying many burdens.
We come wondering if you are even here.
We come seeking your face, seeking your love.
In this moment, Holy One,
open our hearts to the mystery of your love.
Remind us that you are always with us
and that you never leave us.
Reassure us that you love us,
even as you invite us to love one another.
In this time and space, may we say "yes" to you.
In the name of Christ, we pray. Amen.

PROCLAMATION AND RESPONSE

Prayer of Confession (Psalm 27, 1 Corinthians 1, Matthew 4)
Merciful God, as we seek your love and light,
there are times when darkness invades our lives.
Forgive us when we hide our true selves from you.

Forgive us when we quarrel with one another,
    allowing our pride to overcome our commitment
    to the community.
Forgive us when we give life's activities priority
    over following the ways of Christ.
O God, open our hearts to your grace,
    as you once again fill us with your love and light.
Amen.

Words of Assurance (1 Corinthians 1)

People of God, hear the good news of the gospel
    and rejoice!
You are forgiven, and God's grace sets you free
    to love again. Amen.

Passing the Peace of Christ (Isaiah 9)

Siblings in Christ, the light of God shines on us.
The peace of Christ dwells within us.
Share signs of this love and peace with one another.

Prayer of Preparation (Psalm 27)

Holy One, our light and our salvation,
    open our ears to hear your word.
Open our hearts to welcome your love. Amen.

Response to the Word (Matthew 4)

People of God, may these words bring us good news—
news of salvation and hope,
news of light and healing.
And may these words empower us
to share the good news of your gospel.
Christ's love is for everyone.

THANKSGIVING AND COMMUNION

Invitation to the Offering (Isaiah 9, Psalm 27)
God is our light and our love. May we joyfully offer our
gifts to God as tokens of our gratitude.

Offering Prayer (Psalm 27, 1 Corinthians 1, Matthew 4)
Loving God, light of the world,
    we thank you for these gifts.
May they share your joy and your hope,
    bringing reconciliation and help
        to those seeking to walk in your ways.
In the name of Christ, we pray. Amen.

SENDING FORTH

Benediction (Isaiah 9, Matthew 4)
Brothers and Sisters, siblings in Christ,
    may the light of God shine in our lives.
May the love of Christ fill our days.
And may the power of the Holy Spirit
    guide us always.
Go in peace. Amen.

January 29, 2023

Fourth Sunday after the Epiphany

Mary Petrina Boyd

[handwritten: 169 Rejoice Ye Pure in Heart, 21 O for a Thousand Tongues to Sing]

COLOR

Green

SCRIPTURE READINGS

Micah 6:1-8; Psalm 15; 1 Corinthians 1:18-31;
Matthew 5:1-12

THEME IDEAS

God's ways and God's desires turn our human expectations upside down. Micah reminds us that God does not want extravagant gifts. God wants us to do justice, embrace faithful love, and walk beside God. In the Sermon on the Mount, Jesus pronounces blessings on those who struggle: the poor in spirit, the grieving, the meek, the hungry, the persecuted. Writing to the church at Corinth, Paul declares that the message of the cross is foolishness to many, but God's people find deep wisdom there.

INVITATION AND GATHERING

Centering Words (Matthew 5)

What blessings do you need this morning? Where in life are you struggling? God will be there and give you what you need.

–OR–

Centering Words (1 Corinthians 1:25)
The foolishness of God is wiser than human wisdom, and the weakness of God is stronger than human strength.

Call to Worship (Psalm 15)
Come, let us walk in God's ways.
Let us listen for God's word.
We will dwell here in God's tent.
We will sing God's praises.

–OR–

Call to Worship (Micah 6)
What does God require of us?
God wants justice.
What else does God want?
God wants faithful love.
Anything else?
God wants us to walk humbly with God.

Opening Prayer (Micah 6, Psalm 15, 1 Corinthians 1)
Come, Holy Wisdom, and show us your ways.
In our confusing world,
many voices demand our attention.
Teach us to look with your eyes.
Help us walk humbly beside you—
doing what is right, speaking your truth.
You alone are our guide and guardian
on paths of peace and reconciliation. Amen.

PROCLAMATION AND RESPONSE

Prayer of Confession (Matthew 5)
God of compassion, we are overwhelmed
by the struggles of life.

We hunger and thirst for righteousness,
   but find ourselves feeling empty.
We grieve in seasons of loss,
   feeling hopeless and lost.
We want to show mercy,
   but we hold on to old resentments.
We want to make peace,
   but we don't even know where to begin.
Come with your wisdom and guide us in your ways.
Renew us and inspire us to live faithfully,
   as you walk beside us. Amen.

Words of Assurance (Matthew 5)
Jesus speaks words of blessing to those who struggle,
   offering joy and gladness each and every day.

Passing the Peace of Christ (Matthew 5)
Jesus said, "Blessed are those who make peace; they will
be called children of God." Children of God, share signs
of this peace with one another.

Introduction to the Word (Micah 6)
With what shall we approach God? Come with open
hearts to listen for God's word in the reading of today's
scripture.

Response to the Word (Micah 6, 1 Corinthians 1, Matthew 5)
Foolish God, you are wiser than we know.
Where we find struggle, you create blessing.
Thank you for your creative love—
   love that transforms our living.
Walk beside us each day on paths of justice and love.
Amen.

THANKSGIVING AND COMMUNION

Invitation to the Offering (Micah 6)

God does not want extravagant gifts. God wants people who value justice and faithful love, people who walk with God. Let us give freely today so that others may experience justice and love. Give so that others may walk beside God.

Offering Prayer (Micah 6)

Generous God, you give us all we need.
You ask only for faithful living in return.
We bring these gifts to you today,
    that they may support your work of justice.
Through this offering, we commit ourselves
    to do justice, embrace faithful love,
        and walk humbly with you. Amen.

SENDING FORTH

Benediction (Matthew 5)

No matter where life takes you, God is with you.
Go from this place filled with joy,
    trusting the blessings promised by our God,
    the bestower of faithful love.

February 5, 2023

Fifth Sunday after the Epiphany

B. J. Beu
Copyright © B. J. Beu

COLOR

Green

SCRIPTURE READINGS

Isaiah 58:1-9a (9b-12); Psalm 112:1-9 (10);
1 Corinthians 2:1-12 (13-16); Matthew 5:13-20

THEME IDEAS

A call to righteousness and a call to shine God's light unites these readings. Isaiah calls for a fast of righteousness: loosing the bonds of injustice and breaking the yoke of the oppressed. The psalmist proclaims that the righteous shall never be moved but will be remembered forever, they will be a light for the upright. Jesus calls us the light of the world and warns that unless our righteousness exceeds that of the scribes and pharisees, we will not enter the kingdom of heaven. The epistle does not fit this theme but contrasts the spirit of this world and the Spirit of God.

INVITATION AND GATHERING

Centering Words (Matthew 5)
You are the salt of the earth. You are the light of the
world. Jesus says so. Be salty and let your light shine.

Call to Worship (Psalm 112)
Happy are those who worship the Lord
and delight in God's precepts.
They rise before dawn
as a light to the upright.
They are gracious, merciful, and righteous.
They shine their light before others
for all the world to see.
They will never be moved.
Let this be our worship.

Opening Prayer (Isaiah 58)
You do not desire a fast of sackcloth and ashes,
but a fast of righteous.
You ask us to loose the bonds of injustice,
undo the thongs of the yoke,
and set the captives free.
Train our hearts to do what is right, O God,
not what is easy.
May we live our days among the righteous,
that we may never be moved,
but dwell secure in your mercy
and your grace. Amen.

PROCLAMATION AND RESPONSE

Prayer of Yearning (Matthew 5)
Caretaker of our souls, aid us in our quest.
We long to be the salt of the earth
and the light of the world.

We yearn to live with such passion and purpose
that our lives may be like a city on a hill,
resplendent in justice and righteousness
for all the world to see.
Shine through us this day,
for we seek to reflect your glory
in all that we say and in all that we do.
Amen.

Words of Assurance (Psalm 112)
The righteous will never be moved.
Their hearts are firm and secure in the Lord.
May your passion for justice and righteousness
keep you near the heart of God.

Passing the Peace of Christ (Matthew 5)
Called to be the light of the world, see this light in one
another as you share signs of Christ's peace.

Response to the Word (Psalm 112, Matthew 5)
Praise the Lord for the hearing of God's holy word.
Blessed are we when we heed God's precepts
and live according to God's ways.
Let us shine for all the world to see,
for truly we are the light of the world
when we reflect the presence of God.

THANKSGIVING AND COMMUNION

Offering Prayer (Psalm 112, Acts 8)
Radiant One, source of every good gift,
we thank you for the light you shine in our lives;
we praise you for the joy you bring to our hearts.
Receive the gifts we bring before you this day,
that they may loose the bonds of injustice,
undo the thongs of the yoke, feed the hungry,
and let the oppressed go free.

Bless this offering and the ministries it supports,
that your light may chase away the shadows
in places lost to hopelessness and despair.
In Christ's name, we pray. Amen.

SENDING FORTH

Benediction (Psalm 112, Matthew 5)
You are the salt of the earth;
so be salty.
You are the light of the world;
let your light shine.
May your thirst for justice and righteousness
be like a city on the hill that cannot be hid.
Go with the blessings of the one
who makes us salt and light.

February 12, 2023

Sixth Sunday after the Epiphany

James Dollins

COLOR

Green

SCRIPTURE READINGS

Deuteronomy 30:15-20; Psalm 119:1-8;
1 Corinthians 3:1-9; Matthew 5:21-37

THEME IDEAS

Some good news throughout scripture is that God gives us choice. From the one struggling with addiction, to the one seeking freedom from abuse, to anyone seeking life's purpose, the freedom to choose holds redeeming and life-giving power. With this agency, and by the Spirit's help, we may, in the words of Deuteronomy, choose life over death. We may also, as Jesus teaches in Matthew, choose reconciliation with others over destructive pride and self-importance. Thanks be to God for the choices we are free to make and for the path Christ beckons us to choose.

INVITATION AND GATHERING

Centering Words (Deuteronomy 30, Matthew 5)
Surely God yearns, as any loving parent would, that we
choose wisely. In this and in every moment, let us bring
joy to God's heart by choosing compassion for ourselves, our neighbors, and all of God's creation.

Call to Worship (Psalm 119, Deuteronomy 30, Matthew 5)
Come, walk in the way that leads to life.
**It is better to be reconciled with another
than to be proven right.**
Come, choose to live a genuine life.
Life is too short for petty resentments.
Come, walk in the way Christ invites us to travel.
**We give thanks for Christ's way,
and for the freedom to follow!**

Opening Prayer
Open our eyes, Holy Spirit, to your love in our midst.
We give you thanks for the power of our minds
to choose right over wrong.
Guide us now, that this power may not overwhelm,
but inspire us.
Help us choose compassion for ourselves and others.
Teach us to set aside old resentments and grudges.
Lift us, with all earth's children and all your creation,
to aspire to the abundant life Christ brings. Amen.

PROCLAMATION AND RESPONSE

*Prayer of Confession (Deuteronomy 30, Psalm 119,
Matthew 5)*
God of grace and glory, you are ever ready to forgive
and free us from our burdens.

Forgive us for judging ourselves and others harshly.
Free us from the times we have made others stumble.
Forgive us for lifting ourselves up
    by putting others down.
Free us from self-condemnation and regret.
With every breath we take,
    help us choose to live in Christ's ways.
This we pray in your holy name. Amen.

Words of Assurance (Deuteronomy 30, Psalm 119, Matthew 5)
    God delights when we choose
    to leave self-destructive ways behind.
    In the name of Jesus Christ, we are forgiven.
    Thanks be to God!

Response to the Word (Deuteronomy 30, Psalm 119, Matthew 5)
    The choices God gives us have the power to set us free.
    Let us pray.
    God, help us to choose life this day.
    Help us choose reconciliation over our pride,
        self-compassion over self-condemnation,
        committed love over reckless desire,
        and hope-filled friendships over competition.
    Every day, and in each moment,
        teach us, Eternal Parent,
            to love ourselves and this world
                in the way you always love us. Amen.

THANKSGIVING AND COMMUNION

Offering Prayer (Matthew 5)
    These offerings belong to you, O Lord,
        for you are the source of every blessing and joy.

Employ these gifts to build your realm.
Send them into the world to heal the sick,
    feed the hungry, and reconcile us to one another.
By our prayers, our presence, our gifts, and our service,
    make your church a true instrument of peace.
Amen.

SENDING FORTH

Benediction (Deuteronomy 30, Psalm 119, Matthew 5)
Bear witness to the way of Christ.
Go with the compassion of God,
    the joy of Christ, and the wisdom of the Spirit.
Go with God, and Christ will lead you in the way
    that leads to life.
Amen.

February 19, 2023

Transfiguration Sunday

Mary Scifres
Copyright © Mary Scifres

COLOR

White

SCRIPTURE READINGS

Exodus 24:12-18; Psalm 99; 2 Peter 1:16-21; Matthew 17:1-9

THEME IDEAS

God's glory pervades all of today's readings. But how are we to respond to such magnificence? When the psalmist calls the people to tremble and the earth to quake, images of averting one's eyes and falling down in fear come to mind. I can almost see that scene in *Raiders of the Lost Ark*, when Indiana Jones and his girlfriend are the only ones who survive God's mighty presence because they remember to close their eyes. But Jesus invites us to a different response: "Get up. Don't be afraid." Moses communes with God in the very presence of God's glory and receives instruction for leading God's people. The psalmist invites our trembling and quaking in the call to worship and extol God in all of

God's greatness. And even Peter recalls that God's glorious words at Jesus's baptism were words of love and affirmation. May God's glory light our way, call us to worship, and give us the guidance we need to follow where we are called.

INVITATION AND GATHERING

Centering Words (Exodus 24, Psalm 99, 2 Peter 1, Matthew 17)
> With loving hearts and open minds, we come into God's presence. With God's open heart and glorious presence, God welcomes us with love.

Call to Worship (Exodus 24, Psalm 99, 2 Peter 1, Matthew 17)
> Listen, for God is still speaking.
> Look, for God is still present.
> Worship, for God is in our midst.

Opening Prayer (2 Peter 1, Matthew 17)
> God of glory, grace us with your presence.
> Overwhelm us with your love.
> Guide us with your wisdom
>   and fill us with your Holy Spirit,
>   as we worship and praise you this day.

PROCLAMATION AND RESPONSE

Prayer of Confession (Psalm 99, Matthew 17)
> Mighty and glorious God,
>   even as we tremble in your presence,
>   we rejoice in your willingness
>   to live among and within us.

31

Forgive us when we act as if we can separate ourselves
from your powerful presence.
Forgive us when we hide ourselves from you,
forgetting that in you, nothing is hidden.
Lift our eyes to see your glory.
Lift our hearts to receive your grace.
Lift our lives to reflect the mountain of your love,
that we may shine for all to see.
In your glory and grace, we pray. Amen.

Words of Assurance (Matthew 17)
Don't be afraid.
We are beloved children of God
We belong to a God whose love and grace
always draw us to our home in God.

Introduction to the Word (Exodus 24, 2 Peter 1, Matthew 17)
Listen for the voice from heaven—the voice that speaks
by the waters of Jordan and atop mountains on high.
This voice speaks to us still, revealing truth and guid-
ance through the words of scripture and the lessons of
Jesus.

Response to the Word (Exodus 24, Matthew 17)
Do not enshrine these words on a mountaintop.
We will live them on every hill
and every valley of our lives.
Get up. Don't be afraid.
Christ leads the way
on a path lit by God's glory and love.

THANKSGIVING AND COMMUNION

Invitation to the Offering (2 Peter 1, Matthew 17)
As God has blessed us with the glory of love and light, so
God invites us to share these gifts to light God's world.

Offering Prayer (Psalm 99)
Embolden us, Mighty God,
to give us fully as we have received.
Multiply the gifts we return to you now,
that they may empower the lives of many
with your glory and your grace.

SENDING FORTH

Benediction (Psalm 99, Matthew 17)
In God's strength and power,
we go now to serve.
In God's glory and grace,
we go now with humility and love.

February 26, 2023

First Sunday in Lent

B. J. Beu
Copyright © B. J. Beu

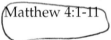

COLOR

Purple

SCRIPTURE READINGS

Genesis 2:15-17; 3:1-7; Psalm 32; Romans 5:12-19;
Matthew 4:1-11

THEME IDEAS

Today's scriptures portray how easily we succumb to temptation and sin. Genesis tells the story of Adam and Eve listening to the serpent and eating the forbidden fruit in the garden. The psalmist tells how happy we are when our transgressions are forgiven and when our sin is covered. Romans claims that just as sin came into the world through one man, so salvation also came through one man, Christ Jesus. Finally, Matthew's Gospel tells of Jesus's temptation in the wilderness before he began his ministry. Temptation and transgression may be ever-present, but mercy and grace define who we are in the life of God.

INVITATION AND GATHERING

Centering Words (Psalm 32)
Happy are those whose transgressions are forgiven and whose sin is covered. Rejoice and be glad, you upright in heart.

Call to Worship (Genesis 2, Psalm 32, Matthew 4)
Temptation surrounds us every day.
**Happy are those whose transgressions
are forgiven.**
Opportunities to stray litter our path.
Happy are those whose sin is covered.
Though we stumble and fall,
God's mercy picks us up.
God's grace brushes us off.
Be glad in the Lord and rejoice,
God's love meets us here.

Opening Prayer (Psalm 32, Matthew 4)
Righteous God, we need your presence in our lives
if we are to resist temptation.
Send your angels to minister to us
when the tempter comes to call.
Put not our hearts to the test,
but shelter us in your protective love.
For you are our God
and we are your people. Amen.

PROCLAMATION AND RESPONSE

Prayer of Confession or Prayer of Yearning (Matthew 4)
God of wilderness wanderings,
many things tempt us;
many forces cause our feet to stray.

Save us from the time of trial,
for we easily succumb to temptation;
we often heed voices that cause us to stray.
Return us to the garden of your abiding love,
for we yearn to walk with you
with faithful hearts and upright spirits.
Amen.

Words of Assurance (Psalm 32)
We worship the one who forgives our transgressions
and covers our sin.
Rejoice and be glad,
for God's mercy is greater than our failings;
God's grace is greater than our sin.

Passing the Peace of Christ (Matthew 4)
Even Christ was tempted in the wilderness. Turn to your
neighbor, who suffers as you do from daily temptation,
and offer signs of Christ's peace.

Response to the Word (Psalm 112, Matthew 5)
Temptation meets us at every turn,
but God is greater than our weakness.
In times of trial, turn to the Lord in prayer.
God will send angels to tend us in our time of need.

THANKSGIVING AND COMMUNION

Offering Prayer (Matthew 4)
Merciful One, we do not live by bread alone
but by every word that comes from your mouth.
Still, we seek your blessing upon this offering,
for many are hungry and need food,
many are naked and need clothes,
many are homeless and need shelter.

May these gifts reflect the depth of our gratitude
as they go into the world.
In Jesus's name, we pray. Amen.

SENDING FORTH

Benediction (Psalm 32)
Go with joy.
Our transgressions are forgiven.
Go with hope.
Our sin is covered.
Go with love.
**Our hearts are uplifted
by the tender mercies of our God.**

March 5, 2023

Second Sunday in Lent

Mary Scifres
Copyright © Mary Scifres

[handwritten:] 401 The Church's One Foundation
[handwritten:] 572 Blessed Assurance

COLOR

Purple

SCRIPTURE READINGS

Genesis 12:1-4a; Psalm 121; Romans 4:1-5, 13-17; John 3:1-17

THEME IDEAS

Our help is found in God. Our guidance is found in God. Our salvation is found in God. This help is a gift born in our lives from above, God's Spirit breathing into our spirits. God's help is as near as our next breath. These gifts—help, guidance, salvation—are offered without price. They are simply given through faith.

INVITATION AND GATHERING

Centering Words (Psalm 121)

Look to the mountains and know this truth: God, our help, is stronger, larger, and mightier than the mightiest mountain. God's help is stronger than any trouble this world can throw our way.

Call to Worship (Genesis 12, Psalm 121, John 3)
God calls with a blessing.
Our help is in God.
God calls with a promise.
Our help is in God.
God calls through our questions.
Our help is in God.
God calls through the Spirit.
Our help is in God.

Opening Prayer (Genesis 12, Psalm 121, John 3)
Spirit of help and hope, be with us this day.
Breathe into our prayers and praise.
Breathe into our spirits.
Breathe into our worship with your promise of help,
    your promise of rebirth,
    and your promise of blessing.
In faith and trust, we pray. Amen.

PROCLAMATION AND RESPONSE

Prayer of Yearning (Genesis 12, Psalm 121, John 3)
Faithful One, you know our fears and our doubts.
You know our hopes and our dreams.
You know our blessings and our curses.
Hold us closely with your love.
Breathe into our lives with your mercy.
For we yearn for the courage
to accept your grace and love.
We long to know your presence
    and to trust your grace.
In faith and hope, we pray. Amen.

Words of Assurance (Psalm 121, John 3)
> God will keep you from all evil
> > and bless you with renewal and grace.
> God will hold your life and lift you up,
> > both now and forevermore.

Passing the Peace of Christ (Genesis 12, Psalm 121)
> Bless one another as you have been blessed. Bless one another with signs of support, peace, and love. Together, let us be one another's help and hope.

Response to the Word (Psalm 121, John 3)
> Lift up your eyes.
> **We know God is here.**
> Listen for the voice of Christ.
> **We will follow where Christ leads.**
> Turn inward and find the Spirit.
> **God's Spirit dwells within our spirits.**
> God is always renewing, helping,
> restoring, and strengthening us.
> **In this renewal and help,**
> **we are restored and strengthened.**
> Let us go where we are sent.

THANKSGIVING AND COMMUNION

Offering Prayer (Genesis 12, Psalm 121)
> God, our help and our hope, bless these gifts,
> > that they may bring help to the needy
> > and hope to the despairing.
> Bless us this day,
> > that our very lives may be gifts of help and hope
> > for your world. Amen.

Invitation to Communion (Genesis 12, Psalm 121, John 3)
> The God who made heaven and earth
> > has created us in God's glorious image.

Come to God's banquet table and partake of Godself.
Remember the blessings we have received
    and the blessings we are called to be.
Come to be blessed.
Come to be fed.
Come, for the Spirit is calling,
    inviting us to be nourished and born anew.

Communion Prayer or Prayer of Consecration (Genesis 12, John 3)
    Bless, O God, these gifts of bread and wine,
        that they may become for us
        the presence of your love and grace.
    Bless all of us gathered here,
        that we may become your very image,
        blessed to bless your good earth.
    Blow through our gathering
        with the power of your Holy Spirit.
    Make us one with you, one with each other,
        and one in ministry to your world. Amen.

SENDING FORTH

Benediction (Psalm 121, John 3)
    As we have been helped,
        God sends us to help God's world.
    As we have been restored,
        Christ sends us to restore others with love.
    As we have received the Spirit,
        the Spirit sends us to share our spirits
        with kindness and compassion for all.

March 12, 2023

Third Sunday in Lent

Sara Lambert

COLOR

Purple

SCRIPTURE READINGS

Exodus 17:1-7; Psalm 95; Romans 5:1-11; John 4:5-42

THEME IDEAS

In the Exodus passage, Moses strikes the rock to deliver water in the wilderness, giving life to the wandering Israelites. The psalmist continues this theme, asking us to celebrate the rock of our salvation with a joyful noise. Water appears again in the story of the woman at the well, whose thoughtful questions help Jesus begin to spread God's love through living water. In Romans, we can be encouraged that suffering may eventually lead to hope.

INVITATION AND GATHERING

Centering Words (Exodus 17, Romans 5)

Water in the desert flows from the rock of our salvation. The living water of Christ is poured into our hearts through the Holy Spirit.

Call to Worship (Psalm 95, John 4, Exodus 17)
Worship the Lord and sing God's praises.
**We come into the Lord's presence
with songs of thanksgiving.**
Make a joyful noise for the rock of our salvation.
We rejoice in our time together.
Drink of Christ's living water.
We thirst for God's love!

Opening Prayer (John 4, Romans 5)
Holy One, we yearn to draw near
as we arrive in this place.
We come to calm our hearts, soothe our fears,
and deepen our faith.
As the Samaritan woman before us,
help us draw cool water from the well of your love,
and help us leave with the living water of belief,
through the power of your Holy Spirit.

PROCLAMATION AND RESPONSE

Prayer of Confession (Romans 5, John 4)
Giver of Life, we know we have shortcomings.
In the depth of our hearts,
we struggle to leave our failures behind.
Teach us that suffering brings endurance,
that endurance produces character,
and that character brings hope.
With your grace undergirding our lives,
grant us the patience and persistence
to claim a place in your holy Kin-dom.
May we become your living water
in the wilderness of this world,
creating space for your hope and faith. Amen.

Words of Assurance (Exodus 17, John 4)
Like the Israelites in the wilderness,
and the woman at the well,
living water is within reach.
We need not thirst for eternal life ever again,
for the well of God's blessing is full
and God's love is poured out for all.

Passing the Peace of Christ (Exodus 17, John 4)
May the peace of Christ surround you with living water
in the wilderness of our lives.

Response to the Word (Psalm 95, Exodus 17, John 4)
O Lord, we listen to your voice, and kneel in thanks.
You are the rock of our salvation.
You bring forth water in the wilderness of our lives.
You are a reservoir of hope in lives yearning for peace.
Bring us once again the living water of your Son,
Jesus Christ. Amen!

THANKSGIVING AND COMMUNION

Offering Prayer (Psalm 95, Exodus 17)
Protector God, we hear your voice
beckoning us to be your hands
and your feet in the world.
Show us a way through the wilderness of life,
with knapsacks filled with blessings
and vessels of living water for a hurting world.
Receive these offerings,
that they may be for others
the blessings we have received from your hand.
Amen.

SENDING FORTH

Benediction (John 4, Exodus 17)

May the Lord of the wilderness continue to share
life-giving waters of hope, love, and faith
in our lives.

May we have the wisdom to seek Christ's gifts—
gifts of love, gifts of hope, gifts of diversity,
and gifts of faith to serve others along the way.

March 19, 2023

Fourth Sunday in Lent

B. J. Beu
Copyright © B. J. Beu

548 To the Deer
591 Have Thine Own Way

COLOR

Purple

SCRIPTURE READINGS

1 Samuel 16:1-13; Psalm 23; Ephesians 5:8-14;
John 9:1-41

THEME IDEAS

Vision focuses these readings. God does not see as mortals see. When selecting Saul's successor to the throne, God instructs Samuel not to be influenced by human beauty. The psalmist teaches us to see God's presence even in the darkest valley. Paul encourages us to be children of light and to do the works of the day, that Christ's light may shine on us. And in John's Gospel, Jesus heals a man born blind, even as the religious leaders remain blinded by their preconceived ideas. To see as we are called to see, God must be our vision.

INVITATION AND GATHERING

Centering Words (Psalm 23, Ephesians 5)
Be Thou our vision, O God. Be our eyes. Be our hearts.
Be the grace that flows through our lives. Only with
your eyes can we see rightly.

Call to Worship (Psalm 23, Ephesians 5)
Dawn is breaking. Christ's light is shining.
The Light of the world shines in our lives.
Put aside the cares of the night.
In the Lord, we live in the light.
Even in the darkest valley, God illuminates our path.
Even in times of despair, hope shines forth.
Sleeper, awake! Christ's light is shining.
The Light of the world shines in our lives.

Opening Prayer (Psalm 23, Ephesians 5)
Light of all lights, be our vision this day.
Open our eyes to behold your glory.
Open our hearts to the warmth of your love.
Open our minds to the flame of your truth.
Open our souls to the glory of living as children of light,
that others may see in our living
the sacred mystery of your kingdom. Amen.

PROCLAMATION AND RESPONSE

Prayer of Yearning (1 Samuel 16, John 9)
In our weakness, O God,
we often fear what we do not understand.
In our blindness, we fail to see others as you do.

Yet, we long to see as you see
and to perceive as you perceive.
We yearn to cast aside the shadows of the night
and live as children born anew
in the light of your love.
Help us behold your glory this day,
that we might reflect your light for all to see. Amen.

Words of Assurance (Psalm 23)
Israel's shepherd is our shepherd.
The Light that leads us through the darkest valleys
anoints us with love,
fills our cup to overflowing,
and brings us goodness and mercy
all the days of our lives.

Passing the Peace of Christ (1 Samuel 16, Ephesians 5)
Look around. Look closely. Do you see Christ's light shining? Greet one another as children of light, for that is what you are when you abide in Christ, the Lord of light.

Response to the Word (1 Samuel 16, Ephesians 5)
The light of the world shines in our lives.
Let us shine this light in the world.
Take what you have heard this day.
Take what you have felt in your bones.
Take what you have perceived
with sight beyond the reach of your eyes,
and live as children of light.

THANKSGIVING AND COMMUNION

Offering Prayer (Psalm 23)
Loving shepherd, gentle savior,
we give you thanks this day:
for rest in green pastures,
for refreshment beside still waters,
for health and wholeness for our souls.
As we rejoice in your goodness and mercy,
we offer you our gifts this day.
Through our offering, may others be blessed,
as we have been blessed from your hand. Amen.

SENDING FORTH

Benediction (Ephesians 5, John 9)
Go forth in the light of God.
We will walk as children of light.
Go forth in the warmth of Christ's love.
We will travel as children of love.
Go forth in the flame of God's Spirit.
We will live as children of the Most High.

March 26, 2023

Fifth Sunday in Lent

Karin Ellis

COLOR

Purple

SCRIPTURE READINGS

Ezekiel 37:1-14; Psalm 130; Romans 8:6-11; John 11:1-45

THEME IDEAS

Death and life dance with one another throughout today's scriptures. From Ezekiel we hear the story of the valley of dry bones, of Ezekiel being asked by God to speak to the breath of new life. The psalmist cries out from the depths of life, places that cause turmoil, heartache, and loss. But even in the depths, we find the presence of God. Paul reminds us that we are given new life and everlasting life through the Spirit of Christ. And the Gospel brings us the story of the death of Lazarus and the despair of two sisters who lost their brother. We also see Jesus weeping at the tomb of Lazarus, a very human moment. All of these scriptures remind us that life is not without death and pain. But with God and Christ by our side, we can experience new life and new understanding.

INVITATION AND GATHERING

Centering Words (Psalm 130, John 11)
In this sacred moment, we look for God and find the
promise of hope, steadfast love, and new beginnings.

Call to Worship (Psalm 130)
Come, all who are weary.
Here, we wait for the Lord.
Come, all who have turned away from God.
Here, we find forgiveness and healing.
Come, all who look for hope.
Here, we embrace God's steadfast love.
Come, and fill your hearts with praise and thanksgiving.
Let us praise God!

Opening Prayer (Ezekiel 37, Psalm 130, Romans 8, John 11)
Great God of comfort and healing,
we come today with many questions:
"How will we survive the challenges of this day?
Can we get through our moments of loss and grief?
Will we be comforted when our tears flow
like mighty streams?"
In the midst of our questions,
we hear voices of assurance and comfort.
"I will put my spirit within you, and you shall live.
With the Lord there is steadfast love.
The Spirit of God dwells in you.
You will see the glory of God."
May these voices remind us of your abiding presence,
and your steadfast love.
Thank you for walking with us throughout our days.
In the name of Christ, we pray. Amen.

PROCLAMATION AND RESPONSE

Prayer of Confession (Psalm 130, John 11)
>O Lord, there are times when we are so lost
>>we forget to look to you.
>Forgive us when we turn away from your love.
>Forgive us when we doubt our own feelings
>>and the feelings of others.
>Forgive us when we forget that your Holy Spirit
>>dwells within us.
>Help us see your love and your presence in our lives.
>Help us trust you no matter what life may bring,
>>and help us follow you faithfully. Amen.

Words of Assurance (Psalm 130)
>People of God, the steadfast love
>>and redeeming power of God
>>is with you today and always.
>You are forgiven. Thanks be to God!

Passing the Peace of Christ (Romans 8)
>The Spirit of Christ dwells in you.
>>**And also in you!**
>Let us share the peace and love of Christ
>>with one another.

Prayer of Preparation (Ezekiel 37)
>Holy One, may we hear your word today.
>May we feel your breath of life in our bones.
>And may we open ourselves to the new life
>>that only you can bring. Amen.

Response to the Word (John 11)
>Jesus, our friend and Savior,
>>we give thanks that you call us to new life
>>and to new possibilities.

May the words we have heard today
empower us to rise and follow you always. Amen.

THANKSGIVING AND COMMUNION

Invitation to the Offering (Psalm 130)
God gives us steadfast love and abundant mercy. Now,
we are invited to bring our gifts to God as tokens of our
thanksgiving and praise.

Offering Prayer (John 11)
Abundant God, thank you for the gifts we bring to you.
May these gifts bring new life
    to those who are in need in our community
        and in the world.
In your beloved name, we pray. Amen.

SENDING FORTH

Benediction (Romans 8, John 11)
Brother, sisters, and siblings in Christ,
    may the love of God, the life of Christ,
    and the presence of the Spirit
    be with you now and always.
Go in peace. Amen.

April 2, 2023

Passion/Palm Sunday

B. J. Beu
Copyright © B. J. Beu

COLOR
Purple

546 I Surrender All
92 O How I Love Jesus

PALM SUNDAY READINGS

Psalm 118:1-2, 19-29; Matthew 21:1-11

PASSION SUNDAY READINGS

Isaiah 50:4-9a; Psalm 31:9-16; Philippians 2:5-11;
Matthew 26:14–27:66 (27:11-54)

THEME IDEAS

Palm Sunday presents worship planners with a quandary: to focus the entire service on Jesus's triumphal entry into Jerusalem or to transition from the parade atmosphere of Palm Sunday to the turning of the crowds, the betrayal, and the passion narratives, and thereby risk losing attendance at the forthcoming Holy Week services. Since Easter makes no sense without Christ's passion and death, this entry includes elements from Christ's passion. Fickleness of heart and betrayal focus today's readings.

INVITATION AND GATHERING

Centering Words (Psalm 118, Matthew 21)
On the back of a donkey, Jesus came to save us. On the road to Jerusalem, Jesus came to heal us. In the joy of laughing children and the shouts of loud hosannas, Jesus came to show us the way.

Call to Worship (Psalm 118)
This is the day that the Lord has made.
Let us rejoice and be glad in it.
Blessed is the one who comes in the name of the Lord.
God's steadfast love endures forever.
The stone that the builders rejected
has become the chief cornerstone.
This is the Lord's doing.
It is marvelous in our eyes.
Line the festival procession with branches.
This is the day that the Lord has made.
Let us rejoice and be glad in it.

Opening Prayer (Matthew 21, Philippians 2)
Blessed One, our hearts sing with the children
when we see you ride into Jerusalem on a donkey.
Our lips shout your praises,
as you empty yourself to become servant of all.
Open our hearts to the depth of your love,
that we might walk faithfully with you
during the long week ahead. Amen.

PROCLAMATION AND RESPONSE

Prayer of Confession (Matthew 26–27)
Righteous One, we often ignore the desire of our hearts.
We long to sing hosannas with a cheering crowd,
but we turn aside at the sight of an angry mob.

We yearn to dine lovingly at your table,
> but we retreat into the courtyard shadows.

We hope to defend the one we love,
> but we succumb to the limits of our strength.

It is so easy to betray you with a kiss.

Forgive our fickle faith
> and heal our hesitant hearts,
>> for our spirits ache to be found worthy. Amen.

Words of Assurance (Psalm 118)

The one the builders rejected
> has become our cornerstone,
> the very foundation of our salvation.

Christ offers us forgiveness and fullness of grace.

Passing the Peace of Christ (Matthew 21)

The Prince of Peace rode into Jerusalem in lowly estate
to bless us. Let us claim our heritage as children of peace
by sharing signs of our kinship with one another.

Response to the Word (Matthew 26)

Merciful God, help us sit silently
> and feel the depth of your love.

Settle our spirits,
> that we might know just how far you go
>> to bring us the cup of salvation.

In the midst of a week of betrayal and denial,
> help us forgive the betrayals and denials
>> we commit in our own time and place.

In your holy name, we pray. Amen.

THANKSGIVING AND COMMUNION

Offering Prayer (Matthew 21)
Thank you, O God, for coming to us in Christ Jesus.
Work through these gifts,
that the world might know the breadth
of your mercy and your grace.
Bless our very lives,
that we might be faithful disciples
and stewards of your love.
With gratitude and joy, we pray. Amen.

SENDING FORTH

Benediction (Psalm 118)
The gates of righteousness are thrown wide.
We go with Christ's blessing.
The path of salvation is made plain.
We will walk in the ways of truth and life.
The cornerstone of our faith is sure.
Our lives are built on the foundation of our God.

ADDITIONAL RESOURCES

Call to Prayer (Psalm 31)
Like broken vessels,
we need God's healing.
Like those who are dead,
we need the quickening of God's Spirit.
Lift your prayers to God
who delivers us from the time of trial.

April 6, 2023

Holy Thursday

B. J. Beu
Copyright © B. J. Beu

COLOR

Purple

SCRIPTURE READINGS

Exodus 12:1-4, (5-10) 11-14; Psalm 116:1-2, 12-19;
1 Corinthians 11:23-26; John 13:1-17, 31b-35

THEME IDEAS

This service follows Jesus's last night with his disciples. As we remember Christ's gift of love, we are invited to listen to scripture, sing the songs of our faith, and share Holy Communion and a foot-washing ceremony. Jesus becomes a servant to his followers—even the ones who betray him, deny him, and run away in the face of danger. Jesus is an example of faithful living in an age of unfaithfulness. The foot-washing ceremony depicts the depth of Jesus's love and offers us a glimpse of true servanthood. Such is the call of Christian discipleship.

INVITATION AND GATHERING

Centering Words (John 13)
> With the Passover table set, Jesus humbles himself as a servant—even though betrayal and denial are close at hand. Watch and pray, that you may be found faithful during the time of trial.

Call to Worship (Exodus 12, Psalm 116, 1 Corinthians 11, John 13)
> Remember the saving love of God,
> for Christ claims us as his own.
> **Gratitude calls us here.**
> Come to the table of grace.
> Eat of the bread of life,
> and drink from the cup of salvation.
> **Wonder invites us to go deeper.**
> Ponder the depth of Christ's love,
> as he washes the feet of his disciples.
> **Love leads us home.**

Opening Prayer (Exodus 12, 1 Corinthians 11, John 13)
> Your love calls us here, Gracious One,
> calling us to dine with you
> and to be instruments of your love.
> Gather us in Jesus's name,
> that we may offer him the full measure
> of our devotion. Amen.

PROCLAMATION AND RESPONSE

Prayer of Yearning (Psalm 116)
> O God, our failings are ever before us.
> We feel crushed under their weight.

Yet in your eyes, Holy One,
we remain beloved children
created in the glory of your image.
Help us see ourselves as you see us.
Only then will we fully accept the gift of grace
Christ offers us on this holy day. Amen.

Words of Assurance (Exodus 12, Psalm 116)
God saves us from forces that would ensnare us,
even the forces of our self-reproach.
Call on the name of the Lord and be saved.

Passing the Peace of Christ (John 13)
As Christ loves us, let us love one another. Share this
love with one another by exchanging signs of Christ's
peace. They will know we are Christians by our love.

Invitation to the Word
With open hearts, listen for the word of God.
With receptive minds, listen for the wisdom of God.
With humble spirits, listen for the grace of God.
Listen . . . for God is speaking still.

Response to the Word (Psalm 116, John 13)
Embrace the living word of God.
May it open our hearts,
enlighten our minds,
and bless our spirits.
May God's word humble us,
that we may be servants of one another
in Christ's name.

THANKSGIVING AND COMMUNION

Invitation to the Offering (Psalm 116)
As we collect today's offering, let us meet our vows of
faithfulness in the presence of God's people.

Offering Prayer (Psalm 116, John 13)
Source of love and compassion,
   you fill us with a deep, spiritual longing
      to touch the joy of your salvation.
May the gifts we bring before you this day
   fulfill our vows of faithful service,
      through Jesus Christ, our Lord. Amen.

Invitation to Communion (Psalm 116, 1 Corinthians 11,
John 13)
Come to the table of grace.
Here we find food that satisfies.
Taste and see that the Lord is good.
Here we savor the bread of heaven.
Lift the cup of salvation.
Here our souls are satisfied.
Come to the table of grace.
Taste and see that the Lord is good.

Invitation to Foot Washing (John 13)
Loving Servant, in the invitation of foot washing,
   the intimacy of this gift humbles us.
Open our hearts in the naked now,
   that we may receive your mercy and your grace.
We come to embrace the mantle of servant ministry,
   that we might comprehend the love that heals us,
      the joy that completes us,
         and the grace that sets us free. Amen.

SENDING FORTH

Benediction (Psalm 116, John 13)
Blessed by God, let us serve one another.
They will know we are Christians by our love.
Nourished by Christ, let us love another.
They will know we are Christians by our love.
Sustained by the Spirit, let us support one another.
They will know we are Christians by our love.

April 7, 2023

Good Friday

Mary Scifres
Copyright © Mary Scifres

COLOR

Black or none

SCRIPTURE READINGS

Isaiah 52:13–53:12; Psalm 22; Hebrews 10:16-25;
John 18:1–19:42

THEME IDEAS

Lament and sorrow flow through this somber day, as
they do through today's readings. Yet, the God of steadfast love and faithfulness undergirds this lament. The
suffering servant's tragic life has purpose; the psalmist
realizes God is present and listening during our desperate pleas of despair. Even as death arrives, Jesus remains
steadfast to the end, giving John to his mother, Mary,
and Mary to John, that they might not be alone in their
grief. Our times of lament and sorrow become bearable
when we remember we are not alone—God is present
and listening.

*(Designate a place for people to share their offerings as they
arrive. But if you collect an offering during worship, collect*

the offering early in the service so people can depart in silence following the reading of Christ's Passion and the Response to the Word.)

INVITATION AND GATHERING

Centering Words (Isaiah 53, Psalm 22, John 18–19)
Sorrowing, sighing, or even crying, come into the presence of God. For God listens to your deepest despair. God cries with you and carries the burdens of your heart.

Call to Worship (Psalm 22)
Cry out and know,
God is listening with compassion and love.
Even when words won't come,
God knows our every need.
Even when death seems all around,
God walks with us every step of the way.

Opening Prayer (Isaiah 53, John 19)
God of sorrows, as we walk this path of sorrow today,
    comfort us in our despair.
Strengthen us and give us courage for the journey,
    for we know there will be times
        when we stumble and fall.
In faith and hope, we pray. Amen.

PROCLAMATION AND RESPONSE

Call to Confession (Hebrews 10)
Draw near to God with hearts opened wide. God hears our prayers and knows our need.

Prayer of Confession (Psalm 22, Hebrews 10)
When words won't come,
    listen to the needs of our hearts.

When sin separates and breaks us apart,
    reconcile us and make us whole.
When despair overwhelms us,
    lift us from the ashes.
When sorrow holds us back,
    place us on your pathways of life.
In loving trust, we pray. Amen.

Words of Assurance (Hebrews 10)
Our hearts are washed clean by God's love and grace.
In this love and grace, we are renewed and made whole.

Introduction to the Word (Hebrews 10)
As these words are read, allow God to write wisdom on
your minds; allow God to engrave the presence of holy
love in your hearts.

*Reading of Christ's Passion and Response to the Word
(John 18–19)*
(Read John 18:1-9)
Jesus says to us, "I am."
In silence, let us reflect on the Great I AM
    who is among us now.
(Time for silent reflection)
(Read John 18:10-11)
Jesus says to us, "Put your sword away!"
In silence, let us put away our own swords
    of discord and violence.
(Time for silent reflection)
(Read John 18:12-18)
Peter denies knowing Jesus.
In silence, let us confess times we have neglected
    or even denied our relationship with Christ.
(Time for silent reflection)
(Read John 18:19-24)

Jesus speaks his truth,
  but his truth is met with violence and cruelty.
In silence, let us reflect on times when our truth
  has been met with violence and cruelty.
(Time for silent reflection)
(Read John 18:25-27)
Peter denies Jesus yet again.
As we hear the rooster crow after his third denial,
  let us pray silently for those who are lost and bereft,
  feeling distant from God and God's love.
(Time for silent prayer)
(Read John 18:28–19:3)
Jesus again speaks his truth,
  but his truth is again met with violence and cruelty.
Let us pray for people who meet violence and cruelty
  simply for speaking their truth.
(Time for silent reflection)
(Read John 19:4-17)
Carrying his cross by himself,
Jesus is taken to Golgotha where the man of sorrows
  prepares to die.
As we think about his lonesome journey,
  let us reflect on our own lonesome journeys,
  remembering that Jesus walks with us.
(Time for silent reflection)
(Read John 19:18-24)
Mocked, stripped, and hung on a cross to die,
Jesus faces his final hours.
(Sing "Were You There," Stanzas 1 & 2
["crucified" and "nailed him to the tree"])
(Read John 19:25-27)
Even in his suffering unto death,
  Jesus cared for his beloved family and friends.

In silence, let us express prayers of gratitude
that Jesus cares for us in our suffering,
in our needs, and in our sorrows.
(Time for silent prayer)
(Read John 19:28-30)
*(Time for Silent Reflection, as a single bell tolls
and candles are extinguished.)*
(Read John 19:31-42)
*(Sing "Were You There," stanzas 3 & 5
["pierced him" and "laid him in the tomb"])*

THANKSGIVING AND COMMUNION

Offering Prayer (Hebrews 10)
As we offer our gifts and our lives back to you, O God,
may they remind us of your great offering of love—
the gift of your Son, Christ Jesus. Amen.

SENDING FORTH

Benediction (John 19)
*(Many churches omit the Benediction on Good Friday, allow-
ing the congregation to exit in silence and experience the emp-
tiness of Holy Saturday.)*
God meets us in the shadow of the cross.
We are there even now.
May the shadow of Christ's love
shelter us in the days ahead,
as we await his joyous resurrection on Easter morn.

April 9, 2023

Easter Sunday

Mary Scifres
Copyright © Mary Scifres

COLOR

White

SCRIPTURE READINGS

Acts 10:34-43; Psalm 118:1-2, 14-24; Colossians 3:1-4; John 20:1-18 (or Matthew 28:1-10)

THEME IDEAS

Jesus is not found among the dead, but among the living. Today's readings celebrate the Risen Christ, reminding us that Jesus is not in the tomb, nor is Jesus earth-bound. Mary isn't allowed to touch her savior as he dwells somehow between earthly death and heavenly life. Angels remind the women that Jesus is not in the tomb but is raised from the dead. Colossians 3 reminds us that we also are raised with Christ. Peter invites us to focus on things above, proclaiming that new life in Christ is available for all without partiality or limitation. Jesus is not found among the dead, much less in the dead ideas that hold us back from the heavenly realm of God's love. When we live in Christ, we live in that realm, here and now.

INVITATION AND GATHERING

Centering Words (Matthew 28, Colossians 3)
Turn your eyes to the heavens. Turn your gaze to hope and life. For in hope and life, we find Jesus, the Risen Christ who shines in our midst with the light of heaven above.

Call to Worship (John 20, Matthew 28, Colossians 3, Acts 10)
Christ is alive,
moving among the living.
Christ is risen,
inviting us to rise in fullness of life.
Christ is calling,
proclaiming life and hope for all.

Opening Prayer (Colossians 3, Acts 10)
Risen Christ, enter our worship and our hearts this day.
As you live and move among us,
remind us to proclaim and live the life you offer.
Inspire us to walk as children of your resurrection,
each and every day. Amen.

PROCLAMATION AND RESPONSE

Prayer of Confession (John 20, Matthew 28)
Holy and loving God,
when we hide away in tombs of death,
lead us into life.
When we cower in our fears and regret,
encourage us with your mercy and your grace,
that we might claim the life you offer.

Help us embrace your love
and live in your risen presence.
In hope and joy, we pray. Amen.

Words of Assurance (Colossians 3)
We have been raised with Christ!
Thanks be to God for this glorious gift.

Passing the Peace of Christ (Acts 10)
Christ's resurrection and life are our peace. Let us share
signs of this life and peace with one another.

Introduction to the Word (Psalm 118)
Listen for the sounds of joyful hope as you receive this
morning's scripture.

Response to the Word (Acts 10)
As children of the living God,
we receive Christ's promise of life.
As children of the Risen Christ,
we give thanks for this glorious gift.

THANKSGIVING AND COMMUNION

Offering Prayer (Psalm 118, Colossians 3)
We give you thanks, O God, for you are good.
You have been our help and hope,
calling us to be help and hope for the world.
You live among us,
calling us to share life and love with all creation.
Bless the gifts we bring before you,
that they may be signs of your life, hope, and love.
Amen.

SENDING FORTH

Benediction (Matthew 28, Colossians 3)
Go and proclaim the Risen Christ.
Go and live as the risen children of God.
Go and be Easter people—
    people filled with hope and life and love
    for all the world.

April 16, 2023

Second Sunday of Easter

Karin Ellis

[handwritten: Fairest Lord Jesus 87 / 493 Glory to His Name]

COLOR
White

SCRIPTURE READINGS

Acts 2:14a, 22-32; Psalm 16; 1 Peter 1:3-9; John 20:19-31

THEME IDEAS

On this second Sunday of Easter, we hear stories proclaiming the resurrection of Christ, the Messiah. In Acts, we listen as Peter reminds the crowd that Jesus, the one raised from the dead, is the long-awaited Messiah, the one descended from David. The psalmist helps us look for hope and joy, as we turn to the Lord who is with us always. First Peter tells us that we have new birth and hope through the resurrection of Christ. And in John, we hear the story of Jesus helping Thomas turn his doubt into belief. The resurrection of Christ brings hope, joy, and new birth.

INVITATION AND GATHERING

Centering Words (1 Peter 1)
Be not dismayed, for Christ is alive, bringing hope and joy to our lives this day. Alleluia!

Call to Worship (1 Peter 1, John 20)
Alleluia! Christ is risen!
Our hearts are glad and our souls rejoice.
Do not worry or fear, for Christ is alive!
In this place, we find hope and joy.
Alleluia! Christ is risen!
Let us worship the one who brings new life.

Opening Prayer (Acts 2, 1 Peter 1)
Life-giving God, we gather today
    to celebrate the resurrection of your Son.
We are grateful for the new life he brings.
We are grateful for the hope and joy he shares.
We are grateful for leading the way,
    as he goes before us.
Gracious God, today and every day,
    we offer you our thanks and praise.
Strengthen our faith,
    that it may sustain us during difficult days
        and enable us to share your love with others.
Open our hearts to new life and new possibilities.
In the name of Christ, we pray. Amen.

PROCLAMATION AND RESPONSE

Prayer of Confession (John 20)
God of mercy and grace, you understand us completely.
Yet there are times when we do not understand
    this life of faith.
We do not understand how Jesus rose from the dead.
We do not understand how the resurrected Christ
    comes to us today.
Moments of doubt and disbelief sap our strength.
Forgive and restore us.

Help us trust you and your love for us.
And help us trust the ways of Christ. Amen.

Words of Assurance (John 20:23 NRSV)
Jesus said to the disciples,
"If you forgive the sins of any, they are forgiven."
Beloved children of God, you are forgiven.
May this forgiveness bring peace to your souls,
your minds, and your body. Amen.

Passing the Peace of Christ (John 20)
Jesus stands among us and says, "Peace be with you."
So, we say to one another:
"Peace be with you."
Let us share the peace of Christ with one another.

Prayer of Preparation (Acts 2)
Gracious God, through the words we speak and hear,
make known your ways of life.
May our hearts be full of your presence. Amen.

Response to the Word (Acts 2, John 20)
People of God, the ways of Christ may be a mystery,
but we are invited to see, to follow, and to love.
May God strengthen us,
as we carry the story of Christ within our hearts
and as we share it with others. Amen.

THANKSGIVING AND COMMUNION

Invitation to the Offering (1 Peter 1)
Through the resurrection of Christ,
we have been given new birth and a living hope.
In thanksgiving and praise,
let us bring our gifts to God.

Offering Prayer (John 20)
    Holy One, we give you thanks and praise
        for your promise of new life.
    We thank you for these gifts.
    As we offer them into your hands,
        may they bring hope and new life
           to those in need.
    In the name of the resurrected Christ, we pray. Amen.

SENDING FORTH

Benediction (1 Peter 1, John 20)
    Members of the body of Christ,
        may the unconditional love of God,
        the deep peace of Christ,
        and the power of the Holy Spirit
        be with you now and always. Amen.

April 23, 2023

Third Sunday of Easter

Mary Petrina Boyd

COLOR *368 He lives!*
White *575 Leaning on the Everlasting Arms*

SCRIPTURE READINGS

Acts 2:14a, 36-41; Psalm 116:1-4, 12-19; 1 Peter 1:17-23;
Luke 24:13-35

THEME IDEAS

The story of Jesus on the road to Emmaus guides this Sunday. The journey was the path that leads to understanding and new life. Holy truth was revealed at the meal. In Acts, Peter invites us on this journey with Jesus. First Peter calls us to live as free people, loving each other, and nurturing the seed of life planted within us.

INVITATION AND GATHERING

Centering Words (Luke 24)
In the midst of confusion and doubt, Love walks beside us.

Call to Worship (Luke 24)
Come walk with us.
We will join the journey.
Let us talk together.
We will listen and speak.
Christ goes with us.
Jesus guides our steps.

Opening Prayer (1 Peter 1, Luke 24)
Holy One, we are often confused
by the events in our world.
Come and walk with us.
Open our hearts to hear your truth.
Plant the seed of new life within us.
In trust of your loving presence, we pray. Amen.

PROCLAMATION AND RESPONSE

Prayer of Confession (Acts 2, Luke 24)
God of love and compassion,
we often fail to understand the truth of your love.
We are frequently confused and filled with doubt.
Life can feel meaningless.
We wander down the pathways of life,
longing to see our way more clearly.
Open our eyes this day,
that we may see your way of love and grace.
Meet our confusion with the truth of your presence.
Feed us with the true bread of life,
and help us change our hearts and lives,
that we may follow you with joy. Amen.

Words of Assurance (Acts 2)
God's promises are for us.
By the power of the Holy Spirit,

God invites us into newness of life,
forgiving and blessing us.

Passing the Peace of Christ (Luke 24)

The travelers greeted Jesus on their journey, not knowing who he was. We too travel together, and there is much we do not know about one another. But this we know: Christ is present in each one of us.

Prayer of Preparation (1 Peter 1, Luke 24)

Open our ears,
    that we may hear your message.
Teach us your truth and sow the seed
    of your eternal, life-giving word within us,
        that we may grow in love. Amen.

Response to the Word (1 Peter 1, Luke 24)

We too have heard your voice
    and know your presence with us.
Give us the confidence to trust your grace.
Help us change our hearts and lives,
    that we may walk with you always. Amen.

THANKSGIVING AND COMMUNION

Invitation to the Offering (Psalm 116)

What can we give back to God for all the good things God has done for us? We can never repay this gift, but we can bring our gifts for God's work in the world.

Offering Prayer (Psalm 116)

God of love, source of all goodness,
    you hear our cries and you answer.
With grateful hearts, we bring our gifts to you.

We bring our offerings, as a gift of thanksgiving
    for your presence in our lives.
We are your servants,
    and we offer ourselves with joy. Amen.

Great Thanksgiving (Acts 2, 1 Peter 1, Luke 24)
May God walk beside you.
    Alleluia! God is with us!
Let our hearts rejoice in God.
    Alleluia! God is good!
Let us thank and praise God.
    Alleluia! Alleluia!
    We will thank and praise God forever!
We praise you, living God,
    for you are the source of all life and goodness.
You called the world into being:
    atoms and molecules dancing into life.
In the glory of springtime,
    the seeds of your grace flourish.
Thank you for new life,
    from blooming flowers to the new hope
    rising within our hearts.
You created humanity
    and set us in a world of abundance.
Yet we turned from your paths
    and became self-centered and greedy.
We ignored the needs of others,
    and forgot to turn to you.
Through the ages you sent prophets like Peter
    who told people to "change their hearts and lives."
Your love for us never failed.
We listen to the heavens,
    as they declare your glory with whirling stars,
    gentle showers, and sunshine.

And so, we join their song
along with the earthly chorus of robins, frogs,
children, and people everywhere:
Blessed is the one who comes
in the name of the Lord. Alleluia!
Blessed is the one who guides our steps. Alleluia!
Blessed is the one who listens and saves. Alleluia!
You, O God, chose Jesus from the very beginning.
He came to walk beside us, teaching us your ways,
healing what was broken.
He opened our eyes to see your love in the world.
Yet his very being threatened the powers of the world.
He was crucified, died, and laid in a tomb.
In three days, the tomb was empty and Jesus was alive.
On his last night with friends, Jesus took the bread,
blessed it, and gave it to them.
This is the bread of life, the very presence
of the Risen Christ.
Then he took the cup, blessed it, and gave it to them.
This is the cup of the new covenant,
overflowing with forgiveness.
At a table in Emmaus, Jesus again took bread,
blessed and broke it, and gave it to his companions,
revealing his living presence.
As we remember these things,
we are grateful for love and new life.
We are yours and we will walk with you.
We remember that the stranger we met on the road
was Jesus, revealed to us in this meal.
And so, we proclaim the mystery of faith:
Christ has died, was crucified, and buried.
Christ is risen and is teaching his love.
Christ will come again to walk beside us.
Pour out your Spirit upon this community,
and upon these gifts of bread and cup.

May they be the living presence of Jesus Christ,
  feeding us with the presence of Christ in the world.
By your Spirit, guide our steps,
  that we may serve you.
We praise you; we thank you,
  for you are our God!
  Amen.

SENDING FORTH

Benediction (Luke 24)
  As you walk the paths of life,
    know that Jesus is with you,
    blessing you with his presence.

–OR–

Benediction (Luke 24, 1 Peter)
  God is planting the seed of new life within you.
  Jesus walks beside you, guiding your steps.
  The Spirit, God's gift, is yours forever.

April 30, 2023

Fourth Sunday of Easter

Rebecca J. Kruger Gaudino

COLOR

White

SCRIPTURE READINGS

Acts 2:42-47; Psalm 23; 1 Peter 2:19-25; John 10:1-10

THEME IDEAS

Diverse believers form the earliest Jesus community through *koinonia* ("fellowship," Acts 2:42). The apostles lead this nascent community in worship and in living *homothumadon* ("together" or "of one accord," Acts 2:46). This formation involves the whole of the followers' lives, from temple to home, with an overarching ethic of generosity toward both God and neighbor. Added to this are the "wonders and signs" of the apostles, which hearkens back to the language of Exodus (cf. Exodus 2:43 and 7:3). The community is involved in liberative work, living out Mary's Magnificat (Luke 1): feeding the hungry and lifting the needy. John writes of the new flock that experiences generosity: a reliable shepherd, safe enclosure from danger, and good pasture. This generous care brings abundant life for the whole community ("I came that *they* may have life . . ." 10:10 NRSV). May we elicit the awe and goodwill of all who witness overflowing *koinonia* in us today (Acts 2:43, 47).

INVITATION AND GATHERING

Centering Words (Acts 2, Psalm 23)
God of goodness and mercy, follow me all my days!
Source of grace and compassion,
    flow from me all my days!

Call to Worship (Psalm 23, John 10)
Hear Jesus's great truth:
I am the gate for the sheep!
We recognize this voice.
We've heard these words before.
Come in! You belong here!
You are safe and cared for here!
We recognize the voice of our shepherd.
Follow and find green pastures and still waters!
We hear his voice.
I come to give life and give it abundantly.
Come one, come all!

Opening Prayer (Acts 2, John 10)
Risen Savior, Reliable Shepherd,
    we hear your voice calling us to follow.
We remember our ancient brothers and sisters
    who gathered in prayer and praise.
Today, we too gather in prayer and praise.
Enliven us with your resurrection power—
    a power that frees us from despair.
Enliven us with your abundant life.
May your living power flow through us
    in all we are and do! Amen.

PROCLAMATION AND RESPONSE

Prayer of Confession (Acts 2, Psalm 23, John 10)
> Loving Savior, Shepherd with the voice we know,
> > be with us when we stray.
> For we often hear the voices of strangers
> > and follow them to dry pastures
> > and dark valleys.
> We forget your voice of love
> > and begin to feel small and lost.
> We fear that we will not have enough to go on,
> > much less have a surplus to offer others.
> And yet you know us by heart and by name.
> Call us once again.
> Restore our souls.
> Walk ahead of us on the right paths,
> > and we will follow you.
> Remembering your voice, we pray. Amen.

Words of Assurance (Psalm 23, John 10)
> Jesus is our gate.
> > **We will enter and be saved.**
> Jesus is our shepherd.
> > **We will walk upon his paths.**
> Jesus restores our souls,
> > **and makes us whole.**
> Surely goodness and mercy
> shall follow us all the days of our lives.
> > **And we will dwell in the house of the Lord**
> > **forever.**

Passing the Peace of Christ (Acts 2, John 10)
> John talks about a flock gathered by the shepherd Jesus
> while Luke talks about a community melded together in
> daily life. Both are visions of the church when everyone
> worships and shares together. Turn to your neighbor

and greet them in the peace and unity of Jesus Christ, Shepherd of the Flock, Shepherd of the Church.

Introduction to the Word (Acts 2)
(The Orthodox Church has a beautiful tradition of bread called the antidoron. This bread is not consecrated but shared with all who wish a cube, usually at the end of worship. Try doing something similar with bread. Have someone cut (with flourish) big, delicious loaves of bread at the Table in front of the congregation while scriptures are being read, maybe even during the sermon. Leave these one-inch cubes in big baskets on the Table for blessing.)

Listen with the glad energy of our faithful sisters and brothers of long ago.

Response to the Word (Acts 2, Psalm 23)
Resurrected Savior, Host at the Table,
Giver of Abundant Life,
    we are blessed to be your gathered community.
Open our awareness to this world of need,
    a world in need of your love and life.
Open our hearts to share the bread of your life with all.
    Amen.

THANKSGIVING AND COMMUNION

Invitation to the Offering (Acts 2)
Some of the earliest memories of the church record acts of generosity, of meeting the needs of any and all. The church earned the goodwill of everyone who witnessed and experienced this gladness. Let us give with open hearts, as our ancient brothers and sisters did.

Offering Prayer (Acts 2, Psalm 23)
(Place the offerings near the baskets of bread. After the offering, explain the tradition of the antidoron: giving to all who want a

blessing of bread from the community. Invite everyone to take a hunk of bread and eat with glad and generous hearts. Encourage people to take a piece of blessed bread to anyone at home.)

God of Abundant Life, Host of our Table,
    we devote ourselves and these gifts
        to your vision of a community
            that meets the needs of any and all.
We give our gifts of money and work,
    of prayer and praise, of presence and purpose
        to our friends and neighbors.
Bless our offering,
    that it may meet the needs, both small and large,
        of your great and generous blessings. Amen.

SENDING FORTH

(Have several people carry the baskets of bread to the doors of the sanctuary. Have toothpicks and napkins ready as people take a piece of blessed bread. Serve any remaining bread in pudding next Sunday during coffee hour.)

Benediction (Acts 2, John 10)

Everyone was struck with awe
by the signs and wonders of the early church.
    This week, let's show signs and wonders
    of our church.
The resurrection power of Jesus Christ,
Shepherd of the Church, is upon us.
    Jesus came that all may have life
    and have it abundantly!
Surely goodness and mercy shall follow us
all the days of our lives!
    May goodness and mercy flow from us
    all the days of our lives! Amen.

May 7, 2023

Fifth Sunday of Easter

B. J. Beu
Copyright © B. J. Beu

COLOR
White

342 Rock of Ages
353 Victory in Jesus

SCRIPTURE READINGS

Acts 7:55-60; Psalm 31:1-5, 15-16; 1 Peter 2:2-10; John 14:1-14

THEME IDEAS

Shelter, safety, and growth in Christ's spirit focus these Easter readings. The psalmist seeks God's refuge and strength against the snares of life. In John's Gospel, Jesus offers assurances that we will be with God, even in death, for God's house has many dwelling places. The epistle reminds us that we are spiritual infants who need the nurture of pure, spiritual milk. If we are to grow like Christ into a royal priesthood, we must become like Christ; we must become living stones within the house of God. Yet, God does not assure us a safe journey. In Acts, Stephen glimpses the heavenly kingdom as the crowd prepares to stone him to death. God is our safety and refuge, but our faith does not promise us safety from the storms of life. It does, however, promise us growth in the Spirit in the midst of these storms.

INVITATION AND GATHERING

Centering Words (1 Peter 2)
> Christ, the living stone and cornerstone of our faith, is building us into spiritual houses and a holy priesthood. Let us open ourselves to the master builder.

Call to Worship (1 Peter 2)
> Once we were not a people.
> **Now we are God's people.**
> Once we ate food that did not satisfy.
> **Now we drink the spiritual milk of our Lord.**
> Taste and see that the Lord is good.

Opening Prayer (Psalm 31, 1 Peter 2, John 14)
> Merciful God, our refuge and our strength,
>> train our hearts on the words of your Son:
>>> "Do not let your hearts be troubled.
>>> Believe in God, believe also in me."
> Feed our souls with your spiritual milk,
>> and build our very lives into spiritual houses
>>> that neither famine nor storm
>>>> can shake the foundation of our faith.
> In the name of the master builder and the living stone,
>> we pray. Amen.

PROCLAMATION AND RESPONSE

Prayer of Yearning (Acts 7, 1 Peter 2, John 14)
Living God, in times of spiritual homelessness,
we long to hear Jesus's assurance
that he has prepared a place for us;
we yearn to be formed by the Master Builder
into spiritual houses, like living stones.
Grant us the courage of Stephen
and the confidence of Peter,
as we strive to be a holy priesthood,
In your blessed name, we pray. Amen.

Words of Assurance (John 14)
Do not let your hearts be troubled.
Believe in God and place your faith in Christ.
Make your petitions known
and the one who is faithful will answer.

Passing the Peace of Christ (Psalm 31)
God is our refuge and our strength. See this in one another as your pass the peace of Christ.

Response to the Word (1 Peter 2, John 14)
Come to Christ, the living stone.
**Like living stones, Christ will build us
into spiritual houses.**
Come to Christ, the Master Builder.
**Truly, God dwells within us,
and we will abide in God's house forever.**

THANKSGIVING AND COMMUNION

Offering Prayer (Psalm 31, 1 Peter 2)
God of overflowing abundance,
    you feed our spirits with spiritual milk
        and nourish our souls with heavenly food.
You are our fortress and our rock
    when the snares of this world
        threatened to overwhelm us.
In gratitude for your mercy and your many blessings,
    we offer you our gifts and our ministries,
        that a wounded world might know your grace.
Amen.

SENDING FORTH

Benediction (1 Peter 2, John 14)
Once we were not a people.
    Now we go as God's people.
Once our souls were parched from thirst.
    But now we go satisfied,
    fed by God's spiritual milk.
Once our hearts were troubled.
    Now they rest secure.

May 14, 2023

Sixth Sunday of Easter
Festival of the Christian Home/
Mother's Day

Mary Scifres

Copyright © Mary Scifres

630 what a Friend
5 71 Trust +Obey)

COLOR

White

SCRIPTURE READINGS

Acts 17:22-31; Psalm 66:8-20; 1 Peter 3:13-22;
John 14:15-21

THEME IDEAS

Living love is an ongoing theme in John 14 and in the
letters of John that appear later in the New Testament.
Today's Gospel reading integrates this theme with the
presence of God's Spirit in our lives. Living love becomes a more realistic possibility when we realize that
the Advocate is among us and within us. Living love
emerges as the most fitting memorial we can offer to
Christ, as we remember his death and celebrate his resurrection during this Easter season.

INVITATION AND GATHERING

Centering Words

God is the creator of all, not just those who claim to be the people of God. God calls and welcomes all of humanity into community. We, who claim our love for Christ, are invited to extend extravagant welcome in both word and action to all of God's children everywhere.

Call to Worship

From the north and south, from the east and west . . .
all are welcome here.
With hands raised high or hearts quietly pondering . . .
we come to worship God.
Bringing our love, opening our minds . . .
**we draw near to God, near to each other,
and near to Christ, the Word of God.**

Opening Prayer (Acts 17, John 14)

God of all nations, for creating us in all our diversity,
yet calling us together in our common humanity,
we offer you our thanks and praise.
Speak to us with your Spirit of Truth.
Reveal to us your loving presence,
and guide us to display your loving Spirit
in all that we say and in all that we do. Amen.

PROCLAMATION AND RESPONSE

Prayer of Yearning (1 Peter 3, John 14)

Spirit of Truth, speak truth to us,
even when we wish to hide from the truth
of our mistaken ways.

Unveil our sins and shortcomings,
    that we might be clothed with your mercy
      and covered with your grace.
In gratitude and love, we pray. Amen.

Words of Assurance (1 Peter 3, John 14)
    Saved by love and covered in grace,
      we are forgiven and reconciled with God.

Passing the Peace of Christ (Acts 17, John 14)
    Extend the hand of welcome to all by sharing the peace
    of God and the love of Christ with one another.

Prayer of Preparation (Acts 17, John 14)
    Ever-speaking God, open our hearts and minds
      to seek your Spirit of Truth.
    Bless us with your wisdom
      and reveal the promise of your love
        through the reading of your holy word. Amen.

Introduction to the Word (Acts 17, John 14)
    Listen, the Spirit of Truth is speaking still with new rev-
    elations and age-old promises.

Response to the Word (Acts 17, John 14)
    As we have sensed God's presence this day,
      we prepare to bring God's presence to the world.
    As God, our companion, walks with us,
      we prepare to walk as companions with others.
    May God prepare our hearts and minds
      to live these promises in the time before us.

THANKSGIVING AND COMMUNION

Offering Prayer (Acts 17, John 14)

God of all creation, you offer us so many blessings.
For creating us in your image
and entrusting us to reveal your presence
throughout the world, we thank you.
Create blessings, even miracles,
through the gifts we now bring,
that others may sense your abiding presence
and know your extravagant love.
In gratitude and hope, we pray. Amen.

SENDING FORTH

Benediction (Acts 17, John 14)

Bring God's loving presence to the world.
Be companions of kindness to everyone you meet.
Go forth, trusting that our companion God goes with us,
now and forevermore.

May 21, 2023

Ascension Sunday

Leigh Ann Shaw

[handwritten: 552 I am Thine O Lord]

COLOR
White

[handwritten: 728 Am I A Soldier of the Cross]

SCRIPTURE READINGS

Acts 1:1-11; Psalm 47; Ephesians 1:15-23; Luke 24:44-53

THEME IDEAS

Jesus is moving upward and the disciples are compelled out into the world. This celebration of the ascension has energy and movement. There is nothing stagnant about faith and this moment has particularly robust energy. Rather than being abandoned by Jesus, the earliest followers of Jesus are commissioned in this moment. This is a time of blessing and joy. This is a time of service on earth for disciples who have assurance that they will be reunited with Jesus later. But for now, there is work to do. Power and energy, trust and blessing, are all embedded in this transition of the ascension.

INVITATION AND GATHERING

Centering Words (Luke 24)
Lifting his hands, Jesus blessed them.

Call to Worship (Luke 24)
Let us gather in this space.
We gather from many places.
Let us center ourselves for worship.
We are one in the Spirit
with joy in our hearts.
Let us receive God's blessing.
God's blessing is ours.
We are God's beloved! Amen!

Opening Prayer (Luke 24)
Breath of God, renew us in this time of worship.
Help us set aside thoughts that trouble us.
Help us pause the challenges of the world that taunt us.
Pour your spirit within each one of us,
    that we may be re-spirited in this hour
        by your power and your grace. Amen.

PROCLAMATION AND RESPONSE

Prayer of Confession (Ephesians 1)
Life-giving God, we receive your blessing,
    but we don't always feel worthy to receive it.
Your call often confuses us
    and your love seems too generous.
We worship and pray,
    yet we still count the times we fall short
        of what we think you expect of us.
Your mercy is abundant,
    but we hesitate to open our hearts to receive it.
Get our attention and draw us closer to you,
    that we may know the relief of your assurance.
As we pray to you, hear our prayers. Amen.

Words of Assurance (Ephesians 1)
God hears our faithful prayers
and looks upon us with eyes filled with compassion.
Christ advocates on our behalf;
through him, we are forgiven.

Passing the Peace of Christ (Luke 24)
We are called by Christ from suffering to renewal, from despair to hope. As witnesses to God's love for all people, let us show God's love for one another. Let us pass the peace of Christ to restore the broken places in our community.

Introduction to the Word (Acts 1)
Open your ears to hear the joy of God's word.

Response to the Word (Acts 1)
The joy of God's word is poured out for us and meets us as we are. God's word is encouragement for days yet to come. May the blessing of God's word sink deep in our hearts and lift us with Christ.

THANKSGIVING AND COMMUNION

Invitation to the Offering
We are blessed by God's word. Let us respond boldly to God's grace with abundant giving for the mission and ministry of this church.

Offering Prayer (Luke 24)
Endless source of life,
pour your blessing upon the gifts
we bring before you.
Bless our giving in your abundance
for the restoration of all people.

Through our offering,
may those who are weary be energized;
may those who feel forgotten find a home.
With the joy of your grace filling our hearts, we pray.
Amen.

SENDING FORTH

Benediction (Luke 24)
Christ is lifted up!
As he withdrew, he offered a blessing.
Receive his blessing today and be commissioned
to serve God in this world.
Offer healing to the broken and care to the empty.
Transform the world through your faithfulness. Amen.

ADDITIONAL RESOURCES

Affirmation of Faith (Luke 24)
We are entrusted with God's Kin-dom.
Just as Jesus led the disciples as far as Bethany,
Jesus leads us to the edge and then sends us on.
We are a community, not abandoned,
but commissioned by God.
We are a community, not broken by the world,
but empowered for our time.
Let us state what we believe.
We believe in God, the creator of the universe:
The one who began the dawn of all time,
the one who sets the time and keeps time,
the one who meets us in our time now.
We believe that all of God's creation is good:
All things that creep and crawl and wander
and roam, God made for good.

All things that croak and moo and chirp
and even whisper, God made for good.
All things that lay dormant or spring up or rest,
God made each one good.
We believe in Jesus, God's flesh on earth:
Our brother who taught us faith,
Our savior who leads us on right paths
when we go astray.
Our Way, who aligns our life for goodness' sake.
We believe in the Spirit, God's energy alive with us
in this precious moment:
Source for all freedom,
the fiery power within and beyond us.
Power that stirs us from complacency.
Conviction of truth that cries for justice.
We believe that every beginning and every ending
is fortified with God's grace.
God is ours and we strain to seek God.
We are the family of the earth,
the kin-dom of creation
In God, we are redeemed and brought home.
Let it be known in us, and in our living,
this day and for every gifted day to come.
Amen.

May 28, 2023

Pentecost Sunday

Mary Scifres
Copyright © Mary Scifres

391 Sweet Sweet Spirit

COLOR *389 Spirit of the living God*

Red

SCRIPTURE READINGS

Acts 2:1-21; Psalm 104:24-34, 35b; 1 Corinthians 12:3b-13; John 7:37-39

THEME IDEAS

These Pentecost scriptures remind us that God gathers us together as one, even as we arrive with different gifts from different places. In our diversity, the Spirit blesses and welcomes us. The Spirit unifies us by inviting us to share our gifts, whatever they may be, and to proclaim our truth in our own languages, whatever they may be. In God's Holy Spirit, the language of love and service binds us together to be one body of Christ.

INVITATION AND GATHERING

Centering Words (Psalm 104, 1 Corinthians 12)
Created by one God, blessed and sustained by one Spirit, all are welcome here.

Call to Worship (Acts 2, 1 Corinthians 12)
Coming from different places,
we gather as one church,
one community of faith.
Bringing different gifts,
we come to offer ourselves as we are.
Blessed by one Spirit,
we bring our unity of gratitude and praise.

Opening Prayer (Acts 2, 1 Corinthians 12)
Holy Spirit, blow through our gathering
as you blew through that Pentecost gathering
so many centuries ago.
Breathe in us your new creation,
that we may be renewed
and revived to be your people once more.
Speak through our differences and our diversity,
and bind us together in unity and love.

PROCLAMATION AND RESPONSE

Prayer of Yearning (Acts 2, 1 Corinthians 12)
Refreshing wind of God,
whisper the truth of your love to us.
Where we are breathless with sin and regret,
breathe new life into us
through your mercy and your grace.
Where we stand firm in our divisions,
re-mold us with your mighty power,
that we might rise in unity and love.
Renewing wind of the Spirit,
help us recognize our gifts,
that we may use them for your glory.

For we yearn to proclaim your presence
in all that we say and in all that we do.
In your holy presence, we pray. Amen.

Words of Assurance (Acts 2, John 7)
All who call upon the name of God are saved.
By calling on God and confessing our sins,
the Holy Spirit re-creates us anew
and saves us by Christ's grace.
Thanks be to God!

Passing the Peace of Christ (1 Corinthians 12)
With signs of unity and love and with God's inexhaust-
ible blessing, let us share signs of Christ's peace with
one another.

Response to the Word (Acts 2, 1 Corinthians 12, John 7)
With many gifts,
we gather as one body.
With different lives and troubles,
we trust in one saving God.
With varied languages,
we speak one truth of Christ's amazing love.
With many gifts,
we go to serve in many and varied ways,
led and blessed by one Holy Spirit.

THANKSGIVING AND COMMUNION

Invitation to the Offering (1 Corinthians 12)
Bring your gifts, whatever they may be. For, together,
we possess all that we need to bless God's world.

Offering Prayer (Acts 2, 1 Corinthians 12)
Creative Spirit, create miracles through the gifts
    we return to you now.
Create miracles through us,
    as we give our lives back to you.
Create miracles through our gifts,
    as we share them with one another.
Truly, the whole of the gifts you have given us
    is greater than the sum of the parts,
        thanks to your powerful presence in our lives
        and in our church. Amen.

SENDING FORTH

Benediction (Acts 2, 1 Corinthians 12)
As you have blessed this gathering,
    bless us as we go our separate ways.
Bless us as we share your gifts.
    Bless us as we live in your presence.
Bless us to be one body,
    even in our different places this week.
Bless us to be one holy Church,
    a church that shares your love with all.

June 4, 2023

Trinity Sunday

Kirsten Linford

COLOR *143 This is My Father's World*
White *147 How Great Thou Art*

SCRIPTURE READINGS

Genesis 1:1–2:4a; Psalm 8; 2 Corinthians 13:11-13;
Matthew 28:16-20

THEME IDEAS

Two themes weave themselves through these texts,
though they appear at first glance to be unconnect-
ed. Genesis speaks of God's acts in the creation of the
world. Matthew's Gospel focuses on the Great Commis-
sion—as Jesus instructs the eleven to go and make disciples of all nations. But these two texts and themes may
be drawn together by the psalmist, who recognizes the
majesty of God's creation and the way that God has put
this creation into human hands. While many interpret
the dominion within Genesis 1 and Psalm 8 to relate
only to power, it is possible to read these texts through a
lens of authority instead—an authority grounded in responsibility and accountability. God calls us to care for
everything God has made.

INVITATION AND GATHERING

Centering Words (Psalm 8)

What are humans that you are mindful of us, O God?
That you care for us? How can you trust us with what
you have so lovingly made? How can we realize that
creation is not only under our feet, but in our hands?

Call to Worship (Psalm 8, Genesis 1)

O God, our God, how majestic is your name
in all the earth!
Your glory shines from below
and grows from above.
You bring wisdom from the youngest
and most vulnerable of us.
You call forth delight in those who live
both long and deep.
We look to your creation and find you everywhere.
We see you in the moon and the stars.
O God, our God, how majestic is your name
in all the earth.

Opening Prayer (Psalm 8)

Great Creator, who are we that you are mindful of us?
Who are we that you care for us?
We don't know what we have done
to deserve your love, God;
maybe nothing at all.
And yet, you give it freely, openly, enthusiastically—
asking only that we receive it,
hoping only that we share it.
Come, and help us receive it.
Come, and help us share it. Amen.

PROCLAMATION AND RESPONSE

Prayer of Confession (Genesis 1, Matthew 28)
Gracious God, you have given us the world.
Yet too often, we have taken it for granted,
    and failed to respect your great gift.
We have received authority
    but thought it power.
We have received responsibility
    but decided it belonged to someone else.
We have received your calling
    but considered it control.
It is easy, O God, to take the power
    and leave the responsibility.
It is easy to forget that disciples are made in many ways,
    not just our own.
We have not always remembered
    that you have entrusted your cherished creation to us.
We have not always remembered
    that the word "entrusted" includes "trust."
We have not always believed that you have trusted us,
    and that you trust us still.
Remind us, O God,
    that we are part of creation,
        not separate from it;
    that we are part of your people,
        not separate from them.
Forgive us when we take your gifts
    and your people for granted,
        and help us start again. Amen.

Words of Assurance (2 Corinthians 13, Matthew 28)
When we forget our blessings,
 we have only to look to God to find them again;
 we have only to remember
 that God already blesses us, already loves us,
 already cares for us.
God is with us to the end of the age.
God's presence will be made full again.
And so will our hearts.

Passing the Peace of Christ (2 Corinthians 13)
The grace of the Lord Jesus Christ, the love of God, and
the communion of the Holy Spirit be with all of you.
Always. Share this grace and peace with one another.

Prayer of Preparation (Psalm 19)
May the words of my mouth . . .
 and the meditations of our hearts
  be acceptable in your sight, O Lord,
   our strength and our redeemer. Amen.

Response to the Word (2 Corinthians 13)
God of Mercy, we have listened,
 and we hope we have learned.
Filled by your love and care,
 we seek now to put things in order—
 to live in peace with your creation and your people,
 and to find your presence in all you have made.
May your word continue to live in us, work in us,
 and make us one. Amen.

THANKSGIVING AND COMMUNION

Offering Prayer (Genesis 1)
You have given us more, O God,
than we could ever repay.
You have filled us in ways
we didn't even know we needed.
Awakened again to both the Giver and the gifts,
we respond in gratitude,
passing along your grace.
Take the offerings of our lives and our hearts, O God,
and use them to care for your family
and for your world. Amen.

SENDING FORTH

Benediction (2 Corinthians 13, Matthew 28)
People of God, receive God's greatest gifts—
gifts of people and place.
Go forth to share these blessings with the world.
Know that the grace of Christ, the love of God,
and the communion of the Holy Spirit
goes with you, now and forevermore.

June 11, 2023

Second Sunday after Pentecost
Proper 5

B. J. Beu
Copyright © B. J. Beu

COLOR
Green

648 Love Devine All loves Excell
856 Take Time to be Holy

SCRIPTURE READINGS

Genesis 12:1-9; Psalm 33:1-12; Romans 4:13-25;
Matthew 9:9-13, 18-26

THEME IDEAS

Faith and grace focus today's readings. Abraham's faith
is exhibited in Genesis and is exalted in Paul's letter to
the church of Rome. In Matthew's Gospel, the faith of
both a hemorrhaging woman and of a desperate father
is juxtaposed with the legalism of the Pharisees. In all
these readings, it is God's grace that makes faith possible. Through this circle of grace and faith, God's miracles enter and bless our world.

INVITATION AND GATHERING

Centering Words (Genesis 12, Matthew 9)
God's grace makes human faith possible. In this circle
of grace and faith, miracles enter and bless our world.

Call to Worship (Matthew 9)
Come into God's presence.
All are welcome here.
Come, saints and sinners alike.
We are all God's children.
Faith has brought us here.
Grace will make us whole.
Come! Let us worship.

Opening Prayer (Genesis 12, Romans 4)
Faithful and loving God,
your grace makes our faith possible.
May we live and go about our lives
as people who place our trust in you.
May we love and care for others
as people who turn to you for help.
Where there is doubt or distrust,
renew our faith.
Where there is fear or insecurity,
grant us courage.
Where there is fatigue and weariness,
give us amazing strength.
Where there is confusion of purpose,
give us wisdom.
Where there is sorrow and loss,
bring us peace.
In Christ's name, we pray. Amen.

PROCLAMATION AND RESPONSE

Prayer of Yearning (Genesis 12, Matthew 9)
Loving God, we yearn to be as merciful with others
as you are with us.

We long to set aside past grudges
    and love others for who they are now.
We are tired of sitting in judgment
    and failing to see others as your beloved children.
Fill us with your grace,
    that we might have enough faith
        to walk in your ways
           and to seek the healing of your world.
Amen.

Words of Assurance (Matthew 9)

By the grace of God,
    our faith has made us well.
In the grace of Christ,
    our faith has led us home.
Through the grace of the Holy Spirit,
    our faith has made us whole.

Passing the Peace of Christ (Matthew 9)

By reaching out in faith, we touch the presence of God. May we feel this touch and this grace as we pass the peace of Christ today.

Response to the Word (Psalm 33)

Righteous children of God, rejoice and be glad.
    We offer God our thanks and praise.
Loving followers of Christ, sing and shout for joy.
    We offer Christ our music and adoration.
Children of the Spirit, skip and dance with faith.
    We offer our lives with awe and admiration.

–OR–

Response to the Word (Psalm 33)

Sing a new song to God.
    Sing with praise and joy.

Rejoice in the Lord of love.
Seek justice and righteousness.
Sing a new song to God.
Sing with praise and joy.

THANKSGIVING AND COMMUNION

Offering Prayer (Genesis 12)
God of Abraham and Sarah, you bless our lives,
that we might be a blessing to others.
May the offering we bring before you this day
be a sign of our commitment
to bless the world in your name.
We send forth these gifts,
that they may be instruments of your circle
of grace and faith. Amen.

SENDING FORTH

Benediction (Genesis 12)
Go to the places God sends you.
Bless the people Christ calls you to bless.
Strengthen the faith of the hopeless and despairing.
Go with God's blessings.

June 18, 2023

Third Sunday after Pentecost
Proper 6
Father's Day

Amy B. Hunter

306 Alas! And Did My Savior Bleed
343 Amazing Grace

COLOR

Green

SCRIPTURE READINGS

Genesis 18:1-15; Psalm 116:1-2, 12-19; Romans 5:1-8;
Matthew 9:35–10:8 (9-23)

THEME IDEAS

How do we respond to a God who comes to us as active, present, and compassionate, yet also as utterly beyond our ability to predict or comprehend? God appears on Abraham and Sarah's doorstep, making an outrageous promise of blessing. The psalmist praises a God who answers suffering and illness with listening and healing. Paul writes of a God who is never out of love with humanity, and who answers human estrangement with divine reconciliation. Jesus looks at the crowd of needy humanity and responds with compassion. Something greater than human metrics is at work. How do we respond?

INVITATION AND GATHERING

Centering Words (Genesis 18, Psalm 116)
Is anything too wonderful for God? What shall we return to God for all of God's bounty?

Call to Worship (Genesis 18, Psalm 116, Matthew 9–10)
People of God, run to our welcoming God.
Holy One, you never pass us by.
People of God, proclaim our love for the God of Love.
Beloved One, you hear our voices;
you answer our cries and receive our praise.
People of God, sing God's good news to the world.
Empowering One, you give us power
to be signs of the kingdom of heaven.

Opening Prayer (Genesis 18, Romans 5, Matthew 9–10)
Loving God, you remind us that the kingdom of heaven
has come near.
Open our eyes, our faith, and our hearts,
that we may perceive and celebrate your presence.
Give us eyes, as Abraham and Sarah before us,
to see you on our doorsteps,
as you promise us unimaginable joy.
Give us the faith of Paul
to trust your eternal and unfailing love.
Give us hearts empowered by your Son, Jesus Christ,
to show your compassion to the harassed
and the helpless.
We ask in the name of Jesus,
who reconciles us to you
and sends us forth to be your reconciliation
in the world. Amen.

PROCLAMATION AND RESPONSE

Prayer of Confession (Genesis 18, Psalm 116, Romans 5, Matthew 9–10)

Ever-present, ever-listening, and ever-empowering God,
we often fall short when responding to your love.
You promise us blessings,
yet we often laugh in cynicism and disbelief.
You always love us,
yet we often act distant and even hostile.
You empower us to be your loving presence,
yet we often seek this power for ourselves.
We call upon you now,
**knowing that you hear our voices
and our supplications.**
We call upon you in this place,
**knowing that no accomplishment
is too wonderful for you to accomplish.**
For there is no limit to your love for all people,
and there is no end to your mercy.
In Jesus's name, we pray.
Amen.

Words of Assurance (Romans 5)

People of God, the Holy Spirit pours God's love
into our hearts.
In Jesus Christ, we share the grace and glory of God.

Passing the Peace of Christ (Romans 5)

Justified by faith, we have peace with God through Jesus
Christ. Let us greet one another with signs of Christ's
peace.

Introduction to the Word (Genesis 18)

Loving God, you have come to your people.
May we welcome your presence and your word.

Response to the Word (Matthew 9–10)
Lord Jesus Christ, this day the kingdom of heaven has come near. May we receive the power of your good news with subtle minds and open hearts.

THANKSGIVING AND COMMUNION

Invitation to the Offering (Psalm 116, Matthew 9–10)
You received from God without payment. Give generously out of God's bounty, living as signs of the kingdom of heaven.

Offering Prayer (Psalm 116, Romans 5, Matthew 9–10)
Loving God, what shall we return to you
for your great bounty in our lives?
Your generosity knows no limits.
Your loving compassion pours into our hearts
and our very beings.
We thank you.
We call upon you, trusting your love.
We offer you all that we have and all that we are,
hoping for your glory
and desiring your kingdom. Amen.

SENDING FORTH

Benediction (Matthew 9–10)
May Jesus, who sees the crowd and has compassion,
have compassion on you.
May Jesus, who sees a plentiful harvest,
send you out as laborers in his fields.
May Jesus, who sees the kingdom of heaven draw near,
make you a sign of God's love for all people. Amen.

ADDITIONAL RESOURCES

A Prayer for Father's Day (Genesis 18, Romans 5, Matthew 9–10)

Loving God, our Lord Jesus Christ called you Father.
Remembering his love for you,
    we pray today for all human fathers.
May they be like Abraham,
    welcoming you with hospitality and laughter,
        and receiving in return a legacy of faith
            for generations to come.
May they rely upon your grace
    as they answer the call of parenting.
And may they show to their children
    the compassion of Jesus Christ,
        who responds to human suffering and need
            with limitless love.
In Jesus's name, we pray. Amen.

June 25, 2023

Fourth Sunday after Pentecost
Proper 7

James Dollins

[handwritten: 686 O God Our Help]
[handwritten: 692 God Will Take Care]

COLOR

Green

[handwritten: Luke 12:22-31]

SCRIPTURE READINGS

Genesis 21:8-21; Psalm 86:1-10, 16-17; Romans 6:1b-11; Matthew 10:24-39

THEME IDEAS

Whether in loss, grief, or a mid-life crisis, we eventually discover that we cannot grasp or control life. It's better, as Jesus teaches in Matthew 10, that we let go of life as we know it and embrace the life God gives. Romans 6 teaches a similarly breathtaking truth, that we are called to die and then rise with Christ. We are challenged to get started today on the eternal life Jesus trailblazes for us. The alternative, holding too tightly to our current lives, can warp us in harmful and selfish ways—like Sarah's demand in Genesis 21 that Abraham expel his son Ishmael, along with his mother, Hagar, from their home. Thankfully, God rescues them, watching over us all as we stumble along in this journey toward grace.

INVITATION AND GATHERING

Centering Words (Matthew 10, Romans 6)
Come into God's presence and relinquish all fear. Let go of life as you know it and discover life everlasting.

Call to Worship (Psalm 86, adapted)
Incline your ear, O God.
Hear the praises of your people.
Gladden the hearts of your servants,
as we lift up our souls to you.
For you, O God, are good and forgiving,
abounding in steadfast love.
In the day of trouble we call on you,
knowing you will answer.
Your people everywhere glorify your name.
For you are slow to anger,
and abound in steadfast love.
Turn to us and be gracious.

Opening Prayer (Matthew 10, Romans 6)
Thank you, Loving Spirit, for the warmth of summer
and for your invitation to embrace abundant life.
Your promise of resurrection allows past troubles to die,
as we rise with you to new life.
Inspire us to follow your lead,
even when it requires us to bear a cross of sacrifice
in your name.
May our love for you be complete,
as we share words and acts of compassion
with a world that yearns for your peace. Amen.

PROCLAMATION AND RESPONSE

Prayer of Confession (Genesis 21, Matthew 10, Romans 6)
Gracious and Loving God, lead us in ways
that lead to life.
Free us to love as completely as you love.
Help us find our worth,
not by lifting ourselves above others,
but by accepting that we belong to you.
May our fulfillment be found,
not in what we hold onto,
but in what we freely give in your name.
Free us, dear God, to live without fear,
following wherever your Spirit leads.
In the spirit of Christ's compassion, we pray. Amen.

Words of Assurance (Genesis 21, Matthew 10)
The one who frees us from selfishness
fills us with God's selfless love.
In the name of Jesus Christ, we are forgiven.
Amen.

Response to the Word (Genesis 21, Matthew 10, Romans 6)
We believe in a God of new beginnings!
**Once, we feared death,
now we look for new life.**
We follow a Savior who carries a cross.
We will carry ours too.
In a world so often governed by self-interest,
Christ calls us to love sacrificially.
Believe in the one true God of new beginnings.
**May our selfish ways die,
that new hope may be born. Amen.**

THANKSGIVING AND COMMUNION

Offering Prayer (Romans 6)
>Generous God, your morning sun gives life,
>>your evening breeze refreshes the soul.
>As life grows to its fullest this summer,
>>let us give generously and repeatedly.
>Through our gifts, may the hungry be fed,
>>the lonely find good friends,
>>>and the grieving find comfort.
>With these offerings, we offer our own lives,
>>that we may rise again to live with you. Amen.

SENDING FORTH

Benediction (Romans 6)
>We believe in a God of new beginnings!
>May the grace of Christ, the love of God
>>and the communion of the Holy Spirit
>>bring hope to our hearts
>>and peace to God's world. Amen.

July 2, 2023

Fifth Sunday after Pentecost
Proper 8

Mary Scifres
Copyright © Mary Scifres

[handwritten: Philippians 1:1-6]

COLOR *[handwritten: 508 Love Lifted Me]*

Green *[handwritten: 512 Jesus is All the World to Me]*

SCRIPTURE READINGS

Genesis 22:1-14; Psalm 13; Romans 6:12-23;
Matthew 10:40-42

THEME IDEAS

Today's scriptures reveal contrasting understandings of
God and the followers of God. Abraham thinks faithfulness means sacrificing a beloved child, whereas Paul
advises us to sacrifice ourselves to faithfulness and
righteousness in response to being saved by grace. Jesus reveals the clearest message. In sharp contrast to
talk of slavery and sacrifice, Jesus invites us to receive
and welcome any and all, for in receiving others, we
are receiving Christ. In receiving righteous people, we
are deemed righteous. Encouraging us to offer care and
compassion to even the little ones, Jesus reveals God's

deepest truth: We are defined by who we love and care for, and how we love and care for them.

INVITATION AND GATHERING

Centering Words (Genesis 22, Matthew 10)
Whether climbing a treacherous path or walking a journey of grace, we are welcomed, received, and accompanied by God. Christ invites us to do the same for others—whoever they are and wherever they are on life's journey.

Call to Worship (Genesis 22)
Come to the mountain of God,
the place of God's holy presence.
No matter how steep the climb,
God journeys with us and helps us along the way.

Opening Prayer (Genesis 22, Psalm 13)
God of ages past and days yet to come,
journey with us today.
Journey with us all our days,
whether on treacherous paths or beside still waters.
Guide our steps to find solid ground,
that we may know the firm foundation
of your constant presence.
Open our minds to the blessings and miracles
we encounter along the way.
In your holy name, we pray. Amen.

PROCLAMATION AND RESPONSE

Prayer of Confession (Genesis 22, Romans 6, Matthew 10)
God of grace and God of glory,
shower us with your mercy and forgiveness.

When we can't see the way forward,
    be our navigation system.
When we make a wrong turn,
    gently correct us.
When we neglect our health and wellness,
    heal us with your love.
When we neglect or harm your world and its peoples,
    reveal your righteousness and guidance,
        that we may be forgiven and reconciled
            with you and with your beloved creation.
Amen.

Words of Assurance (Romans 6)
    In Christ, we are set free.
    We are reconciled through the power of love and grace.
    Thanks be to God.

Passing the Peace of Christ (Matthew 10)
    Receive your sisters and brothers with love. Welcome
    one another with friendship and peace.

Prayer of Preparation (Genesis 22, Psalm 13)
    God of ages past and days yet to come,
        be present with us this day.
    Answer our questions and reveal your wisdom.
    Restore our vision,
        that we may know your presence
            and sense your guiding light. Amen.

Response to the Word (Matthew 10)
    May we be people who receive others with love.
        May we be people who welcome all,
        from the greatest to the least.
    May we be righteous in love
    and generous in compassion.
        May we reflect Christ's presence
        for all to see.

THANKSGIVING AND COMMUNION

Invitation to the Offering (Matthew 10)
Even a cup of cold water can be an offering beyond price on a hot day. May we bring our gifts, whether small or large, to be offerings of grace for those in need of God's love.

Offering Prayer (Romans 6, Matthew 10)
God of love and grace, bless these gifts
with your love and grace.
Through our ministries and our generosity,
may others know your loving welcome
and your gracious mercy. Amen.

Invitation to Communion (Matthew 10)
Come to the table of grace.
All are welcome here.
Come, all who thirst for God.
All are welcome here.
Come, all who hunger for love.
All are welcome here.
Come to the table of grace.
Here, God nourishes our souls.

SENDING FORTH

Benediction (Matthew 10)
As we have been received in God's love,
we go to receive others in love.
As we have been welcomed with God's grace,
we go to welcome the world with grace.

July 9, 2023

Sixth Sunday after Pentecost
Proper 9

Michael Beu
Copyright © Michael Beu

[handwritten: Phil 1:21-30]
[handwritten: 636 I Must Tell Jesus]

COLOR

Green

[handwritten: 581 Tis So Sweet]

SCRIPTURE READINGS

Genesis 24:34-38, 42-49, 58-67; Psalm 45:10-17;
Romans 7:15-25a; Matthew 11:16-19, 25-30

THEME IDEAS

Genesis recounts the story of Isaac and Rebekah. Abraham's servant travels to find a wife for Isaac, and with the blessing of her family, Rebekah travels from her home to marry him. Paul delights in God's law, even as he struggles to live the demands of righteousness. Jesus calls us to bear the yoke of God's love, promising a light burden, even as he laments his rejection by the very people he is called to save. Forgiveness is offered through God's gentle and gracious heart. In Matthew's Gospel, Jesus laments how often we turn away from God and from God's wisdom.

INVITATION AND GATHERING

Centering Words (Matthew 11)
Embrace the yoke of Christ's love. For Christ's yoke is easy and his burden is light.

Call to Worship (Matthew 11)
Christ calls those who are weary and heavy laden.
In Christ, we find rest.
Christ calls us to bear his yoke and learn from him.
In Christ, we see God's ways.
Christ is gentle and humble in heart.
In Christ, we know God's love.
Come, for Christ calls us here.

Opening Prayer (Matthew 11)
You have walked many miles with us, O God.
You have comforted and strengthened us
along the way.
Keep us on your path,
for we easily lose our way.
As we learn to live in your ways,
help us choose the cause
of justice and righteousness. Amen.

PROCLAMATION AND RESPONSE

Prayer of Confession (Romans 7, Matthew 11)
Merciful God, we do not understand
why we do the things we do.
Forgive our foolish ways.
Give us the strength and the courage
to bear your yoke and to heed your call.
In Christ's name, we pray. Amen.

Words of Assurance (Romans 7, Matthew 11)
Christ rescues us from our foolish ways
and from our misguided deeds.
In Christ, we are made perfect,
even in our imperfection.
Thanks be to God.

Passing the Peace of Christ (Matthew 11)
Christ offers us God's gentle and humble heart. May we in turn offer our gentle and humble hearts to one another with signs of love and peace.

Response to the Word (Genesis 24, Romans 7, Matthew 11)
When Abraham and Sarah heard God's call,
they traveled to where God led.
When Isaac and Rebekah heard God's call,
Rebekah traveled to Isaac as God led.
The God of our ancestors calls to us now.
We will travel where God leads.
Thanks be to God, who strengthens us
for the journey of faith.

THANKSGIVING AND COMMUNION

Invitation to the Offering (Genesis 24, Matthew 11)
Isaac offered gifts to show his commitment to Rebekah, and Rebekah responded with faithful love. May we respond to God's commitment with faithful love to those who are in need of our gifts this day.

Offering Prayer (Psalm 45)
    Generous God, may these gifts celebrate your name
        among the nations.
    May the lives we live celebrate your name
        for all time and all generations.
    Receive these offerings as signs of our praise,
        both now and forevermore. Amen.

SENDING FORTH

Benediction (Genesis 24, Romans 7, Matthew 11)
    Go forth with the confidence of Rebekah,
        who left everything behind to follow God.
    Go forth with the delight of Paul,
        who felt freedom to follow Christ.
    Go forth with the joy of the Holy Spirit,
        who dances with praise throughout creation.

July 16, 2023

Seventh Sunday after Pentecost
Proper 10

Sara Lambert

[handwritten: Phil 2:1-13]

COLOR
Green

[handwritten: 52 O For A Thousand]
[handwritten: 130 Stand Up Stand Up]

SCRIPTURE READINGS

Genesis 25:19-34; Psalm 119:105-112; Romans 8:1-11; Matthew 13:1-9, 18-23

THEME IDEAS

The Parable of the Sower in Matthew teaches us to nurture the soil of our lives, as we listen to the word of God for understanding and action. As seeds are scattered near the path, we can count on the word of God as a lamp to our feet, lighting the path for even greater understanding. Taking those ideas into the world, we can learn to nurture ourselves as well as others.

INVITATION AND GATHERING

Centering Words (Matthew 13, Psalm 119)
When you allow God's word to shed light along your garden paths, you prepare the soil of your life to produce

beautiful, healthy growth. May you see the light God, feel the warmth of the Son, and hear the Spirit in the music of the wind.

Call to Worship (Matthew 13, Psalm 119)
Come in from busy, summertime days
to this place of worship.
We come to connect with God's word.
Come in from the stress of everyday life
into the light of knowledge.
We come as seekers of truth.
Come into worship with offerings of praise.
We come to hear the word and respond!

Opening Prayer (Matthew 13, Psalm 119)
Loving God, gather us into this moment of reverence,
celebration, and growth.
As your sons and daughters,
we long for renewed faith
and meaning in our lives.
Christ's Parable of the Sower lights our path,
with its images of rocky ground, tangled thorns,
and green shoots.
May the light of your word illuminate our way
and become the joy of our hearts! Amen.

PROCLAMATION AND RESPONSE

Prayer of Yearning (Matthew 13, Psalm 119)
Merciful One, we often feel the burden of living,
as though we've been tossed on rocky soil
and left to struggle on our own.
Other days, we throw ourselves too quickly
onto wrong paths.

We are tested by hungry birds;
  we are choked by thorns,
    and wither in the beating sun.
We are here to choose different paths,
    confirm new oaths, admit our afflictions,
      and ask you to give us life again.
Perfect One, show us your ways
    and bless us with your sacraments,
      that we may not stray from your road.
Help us hear your word, understand it,
    and bear your fruit for the world.

Words of Assurance (Matthew 13, Psalm 119)
  Be assured that it's never too late!
  The God of Love, and Christ the storyteller,
    remind us to listen, understand, and act.
  Prepare your hearts as garden beds for God's seeds
    of joy and hope.
  Receive God's grace today and every day.

Passing the Peace of Christ (Matthew 13)
  May the peace of Christ bring you budding blooms of
  faith.

Response to the Word (Matthew 13, Psalm 119)
  Once again, we hear your word today, O God.
  As we strive to take it in and make it our own,
    help us respond as you need.
  Prepare the soil of our lives,
    that it be fertile ground,
      as we go to share your word.
  For you are joy; you are hope; you are life.

THANKSGIVING AND COMMUNION

Offering Prayer (Matthew 13, Psalm 119)
Just as your word is a light to our path, Holy One,
may our offering of praise be a light to the world.
In this season of fruitful gardens,
help us share bountiful harvests
of our own making.
Whether our offering be of our time, wealth, or prayer,
receive and multiply our gifts
through the glory of your love. Amen.

SENDING FORTH

Benediction (Matthew 13, Psalm 119)
May your path be gentle, your soil rich,
and your weeds small.
As you go forth into the world,
look for gardens to water, feed, and cultivate.
Nurture the love of Christ in others,
as well as in yourselves. Amen!

July 23, 2023

Eighth Sunday after Pentecost
Proper 11

B. J. Beu
Copyright © B. J. Beu

COLOR

Green

[handwritten: Phil 4:1-9]
[handwritten: 150 Peace Like A River]
[handwritten: 705 It is Well]

SCRIPTURE READINGS

Genesis 28:10-19a; Psalm 139:1-12, 23-24;
Romans 8:12-25; Matthew 13:24-30, 36-43

THEME IDEAS

The theme of God's searching love unfolds and deepens
with each reading. As he sleeps, Jacob dreams of a ladder rising to heaven with angels of the Lord ascending
and descending its rungs. The psalmist proclaims that
God pursues us everywhere, from the farthest reaches
of the sea to the very depths of Sheol. Paul urges us to
give thanks for life in the Spirit by living as children of
God, rather than as children of the flesh. Jesus tells his
disciples the parable of the wheat and the tares to remind them that though children of darkness surround
us, our task is to focus on living as children of light.

God's salvific love does not exist in one spot of hallowed ground in the desert, it pursues us every minute of every day. God's searching love heals us and the rest of creation, making us children of adoption, children of the Most High. Our proper response to such love is deep gratitude, not hostility to those who have yet to find their way.

INVITATION AND GATHERING

Centering Words (Genesis 28, Psalm 139)
In this house of God, angels traverse ladders of holy love. Surely the presence of the Lord is in this place.

Call to Worship (Genesis 28, Psalm 139)
This is none other than the house of God.
This is nothing less than the gate of heaven.
Surely the presence of the Lord is in this place.
God hems us in, behind and before,
and lays hands of blessing upon us.
Such knowledge is too wonderful for us.
It is so high we cannot attain it.
Rest in the majesty of our God.
Give thanks and sing of God's glory.
Surely the presence of the Lord is in this place.

Opening Prayer (Genesis 28, Psalm 139)
Caretaker of our souls, you search us and know us;
you are acquainted with all of our ways.
Your Spirit hems us in, behind and before.
You discern our thoughts from afar.
If we take the wings of the morning
and settle at the farthest limits of the sea,
even there your hand shall lead us,
and your might shall hold us fast.

How can we bear such wonder?
How can we fathom such awe and splendor?
Breathe your Spirit upon us,
    and claim us as children of light,
        that we might be found worthy
           of your love and care. Amen.

PROCLAMATION AND RESPONSE

Prayer of Yearning (Psalm 139, Romans 8, Matthew 13)
Holy Mystery, we yearn to grow closer to you this day.
When our spirits grow unsettled
    and groan in travail like our warming planet,
        meet us in our need.
When we seek isolation from the rancor of our time,
    remind us how the wheat and weeds grow together
        until the harvest.
When we feel captive to the pressures of this world,
    remind us that we need not succumb to our fears,
        for you have given us a spirit of adoption
           as children of God.
Pursue us and hold us near, Gentle One,
    that we may truly be set free. Amen.

Words of Assurance (Psalm 139)
The one who hems us in, behind and before,
    loves us with a fierce tenderness.
The one who pursues us to the farthest limit of the sea,
    fills us with peace and grace beyond measure.

Passing the Peace of Christ (Romans 8)
As children of light who have been adopted into the family of God, greet one another with joy by sharing signs of Christ's peace.

Response to the Word (Matthew 13)
God of overflowing abundance,
   you cause the sun to shine
      on the righteous and the unrighteous;
   you cause the rain to fall
      on the just and the unjust.
Grant us the spaciousness of mind
   to accept the weeds that grow in our lives,
      lest we uproot the good with the bad.
In your holy wisdom, we pray. Amen.

THANKSGIVING AND COMMUNION

Offering Prayer (Genesis 28)
God of dreams and visions,
   we offer you our gifts this day
      in gratitude and praise for your angels
         who come to bring us your blessings.
May this offering be a sign of our commitment
   to be a blessing to all the peoples of the earth.
Amen.

SENDING FORTH

Benediction (Genesis 28, Romans 8)
Keep your eyes on the gate of heaven.
   We will see angels climbing Jacob's ladder,
   as they bring our prayers to God.
Fix your gaze on the entry to the Holy One.
   We will see angels climbing Jacob's ladder,
   as they bring our hopes before the Lord.
Wherever you are on life's journey,
   take time to mark sacred encounters with joy.
   We will see the salvation of our God.
Go as children of light, children of the living God.

July 30, 2023

Ninth Sunday after Pentecost
Proper 12

Michael Beu
Copyright © Michael Beu

COLOR

Green

SCRIPTURE READINGS

Genesis 29:15-28; Psalm 105:1-11, 45b; Romans 8:26-39; Matthew 13:31-33, 44-52

THEME IDEAS

Today's scriptures embody the lesson: "Good things come to those who wait." God's realm is worth waiting for. It is certainly worth the hard work to bring it to fruition. Whether we are working on behalf of a beloved friend, or we are trusting Christ to get us through times of hardship; whether we are awaiting spring to bloom from small seeds, or we are toiling for the sake of love, such work is always worthwhile. When love bursts forth in tangible and life-giving ways, it is always worth the wait.

INVITATION AND GATHERING

Centering Words
Good things come to those who wait. Like seeds buried
in the ground, God's love bursts forth in the fullness of
time to bring new life and new possibilities.

Call to Worship (Psalm 105, Romans 8)
Sing God's praise.
Give thanks to the Lord above.
Seek the Lord and trust God's strength.
Proclaim God's wonderful works.
Live in the Spirit of love and grace.
Give thanks for Christ's marvelous love.

Opening Prayer (Romans 8, Matthew 13)
Spirit of God, you intercede for us
with sighs too deep for words.
When all seems lost, you heal our hearts
and give us strength to carry on.
Set our hearts and minds on you, Great Spirit,
that we may know your abiding presence
and your never-failing love. Amen.

PROCLAMATION AND RESPONSE

Prayer of Yearning (Psalm 105, Romans 8, Matthew 13)
Loving God, as we seek you,
search our hearts and ease our troubled spirits.
Where we are frightened and unsure of your love,
restore us with the assurance of your grace.
Even when we give up too easily,
we long for the courage
to reach for new beginnings.

We yearn to know deep in our bones
that nothing in heaven or on earth
can separate us from your great love. Amen.

Words of Assurance (Romans 8)
Remember, beloved children of God,
neither height nor depth,
nor anything else in all creation,
can separate us from the love of God.
Give thanks to God for this marvelous gift.

Passing the Peace of Christ (Romans 8, Matthew 13)
As we wait and work to bring God's realm, let us offer signs of our hope by sharing the peace of Christ with one another.

Response to the Word (Genesis 29, Psalm 105, Matthew 13)
God molds us into people of possibility.
We will watch and wait
for God's help and guidance.
Christ plants seeds of life with us,
that we may grow with the vigor of his love.
The Spirit nourishes us,
that we may bring forth the kingdom.

THANKSGIVING AND COMMUNION

Invitation to the Offering (Psalm 105)
Let us share our gifts to make God's deeds known among the peoples. May our gifts and offerings glorify God and tell of Christ's wonderful works.

Offering Prayer (Psalm 105, Matthew 13)
God, you bless us with gifts of love
and moments of grace and mercy.
For this earth and its bounty,
we give you our thanks.
For our lives and for the opportunity
to share them with those we love,
we offer you our praise.
Bless the gifts we lay before you,
that they may be signs of your loving kingdom
to a world awaiting good news.

SENDING FORTH

Benediction (Romans 8, Matthew 13)
If God is for us, what more do we need?
Nothing can separate us
from Christ's gracious love.
If Christ is with us, what can stop us?
Nothing can keep us from sharing
Christ's gifts of love and strength.
Go with love as our guide.
God is our constant companion.

August 6, 2023

Tenth Sunday after Pentecost
Proper 13

B. J. Beu
Copyright © B. J. Beu

COLOR

Green

688 Savior Like a Shepherd

488 Just As I Am

SCRIPTURE READINGS

Genesis 32:22-31; Psalm 17:1-7, 15; Romans 9:1-5;
Matthew 14:13-21

THEME IDEAS

Doubt, faith, and blessing weave today's scriptures together. Jacob doubts he can cross Esau's land without
being attacked, so he sends his family and flocks ahead.
When confronted by an angel, Jacob is not cowed by
his lack of faith, demanding instead to be blessed. Paul
has no doubt that God has called him to preach to the
Gentiles, yet this does not annul the blessings God has
bestowed upon Israel. And while Jesus's disciples want
to send the crowds away for food, Jesus knows that they
themselves could bless the hungry followers with food
if they had sufficient faith. Even in our doubts, blessings

are to be had through the one from whom all blessings flow. An additional theme is seeing God face to face, as Jacob struggles with the angel. The psalmist is confident in seeing God's face in righteousness.

INVITATION AND GATHERING

Centering Words (Genesis 32)
When our faith is at its weakest, God struggles with us—not to punish, but to bless us, if we have the courage to ask.

Call to Worship (Matthew 14)
Are you hungry for a word of hope?
We come to be fed and nourished.
Are you yearning to see the bounty of God?
We long to see and believe.
Are you ready to witness the power of our God?
We are ready.
Come! Let us worship.

Opening Prayer (Genesis 32)
Even when our faith falters,
we will not let you go, O God.
Even though we are ashamed by our lack of faith,
we will not let you go.
Because you meet us in our utmost need,
we will not let you go.
Strive with us until dawn, O Lord,
we will not let you go.
We need your blessing now more than ever.
we will not let you go. Amen.

PROCLAMATION AND RESPONSE

Prayer of Yearning (Genesis 32, Matthew 14)
God of wonder and mystery,
    you struggle with us when our faith is weakest,
        yet you do not overcome us;
    you meet us in our weakness,
        yet you do not humble us with your strength.
In dark nights of the soul,
    and when the needs of others seem too great,
        you always stand us back on our feet.
When we face overwhelming odds
    and yearn to find an easy way out,
        you open new vistas of faithful living.
Stay with us when we have need of you, O God,
    and bless us in our struggles,
        that we might be a blessing for others in need.
Amen.

Words of Assurance (Psalm 17, Matthew 14)
Christ's grace is sufficient to meet every need.
Rejoice and meet your God face to face,
    as you receive the bounty of God's hand.

Passing the Peace of Christ (Psalm 17, Matthew 14)
In times of plenty and want, God meets us in our need.
As sisters and brothers in Christ, let us turn and draw
strength from one another, by sharing signs of Christ's
peace.

Response to the Word (Genesis 32, Psalm 17, Matthew 14)
Fed on the wisdom of God's word,
    let us strive toward the goal
    of seeing God face to face.

May God touch our minds with understanding,
that we may sense Christ's presence
in the struggles and wounds of life. Amen.

THANKSGIVING AND COMMUNION

Invitation to the Offering (Matthew 14)
Faced with a hungry crowd and only five loaves and
two fish, Jesus fed the multitude until all were satisfied.
Faced with a hungry world, God invites us to offer our
gifts, that God's bounty may be shared with those in
need. May Christ see our faith and multiply our gifts,
that all might be satisfied.

Offering Prayer (Matthew 14)
Source of Compassion, you meet our needs.
May our gifts become loaves and fish
for those who hunger.
May our offerings become love and light
for those who feel lost and afraid.
Bless our lives and our ministries,
that we may be a people who share our abundance
with those who live in want.
In our living and in our giving,
may the world be fed and made whole again.
Amen.

Invitation to Communion (Matthew 14)
Eternal God, we are hungry in body and spirit.
We are empty and long to be filled.
We are hungry and long to be fed.
We are lost and long to be found.

Heal our brokenness through the breaking of this bread
and the sharing of this cup.
Then pick up the pieces of our lives,
just as Jesus gathered up the fragments
of bread and fish after he fed the five thousand.

SENDING FORTH

Benediction (Genesis 32)
We are blessed by the hand that leads us
to a land flowing with milk and honey.
We go with God's blessings.
We are blessed by the one who heals our wounds
and makes us whole.
**We go with the blessings of the one
who meets us face to face.**

August 13, 2023

Eleventh Sunday after Pentecost
Proper 14

Silvia Purdie

COLOR *444 I Love to Tell the Story*
Green *11 Come Thou Font of Every Blessing*

SCRIPTURE READINGS

Genesis 37:1-4, 12-28; Psalm 105:1-6, 16-22, 45b;
Romans 10:5-15; Matthew 14:22-33

THEME IDEAS

Anxiety is an increasingly prevalent part of life in the world today. What was experienced by the disciples in the wind and the waves and the dark of night resonates with our experience of anxiety in a world tossed by threats of climate change, upheaval, and pandemic. The pit into which Joseph was pushed is another powerful metaphor for the dark places of life, which often manifest as mental illness. Worship is a wonderful space to hear the words of Jesus: "Take heart, it is I; do not be afraid" (Matthew 14:27 NRSV). In prayer, we can receive these words deep in our souls.

147

INVITATION AND GATHERING

Centering Words (Matthew 14:27 NRSV)
Jesus called to his friends as they were rocked by fear:
"Take heart, it is I; do not be afraid." Find shalom and
rest in the midst of daily anxiety.

Call to Worship (Psalm 105)
O give thanks to the Lord!
Holy One, we come with thanks on our lips.
Sing to God, sing praises!
Rise up your song in our souls.
Tell of God's wonderful works!
Our hearts find joy in seeking you.
Seek the Lord and claim God's strength!
We grow strong in your power and might.
Remember all that God has done!
You shape our lives through every challenge.
Praise the Lord!
We praise you, Lord!

*Opening Prayer (Genesis 37, Psalm 105, Romans 10:15
NRSV, Matthew 14)*
Eternal God, in visions and dreams,
    you offer us hope for a new tomorrow.
Amidst life's storms and raging waters,
    be with us in our time of need.
Reveal to us the great works we are capable of,
    that we may rise above our narrow purposes,
        and be of service to the world.
Bless our journeys,
    that it may be said of us:
        "How beautiful are the feet
            of those who bring good news!"
(B. J. Beu)

PROCLAMATION AND RESPONSE

Prayer of Confession (Genesis 37)
We hear this morning the dramatic story of Joseph being thrown into a pit and then sold into slavery by his brothers. We too have known what it is to be betrayed. We too have known the feel of a pit, of being trapped and afraid. We too have been pulled in directions we do not wish to go. As we hear Joseph's story this morning, we honor our own stories of pain and grief. Let us pray.
Lord of all our journeys, like Joseph's brothers,
    we too find expedient ways
        to get rid of our problems;
    we too have cracks in our own families
        that deepen with every unkind word
            and the rejection of those we should love.
God of hope, like Joseph,
    we too can find ourselves victims of violence,
        trapped in the dark, dragged against our will;
    we too can feel abandoned
        by those who should love us.
In this quiet space of worship,
    we gather up every thread of pain
        and lay them in your warm embrace,
            placing our trust in you alone.

(Pause for a moment of silence)

We are your family.
We belong to you.
Wash us in your forgiveness and your strength
    and hold us in your love. Amen.

Assurance of Pardon (Romans 10, Matthew 14)
Everyone who calls on the name of the Lord
    will be saved.

Everyone who risks the uncertain walk of faith
   receives aid from the one who calms the waters.
(B. J. Beu)

Passing the Peace of Christ (Genesis 37, Romans 10)
   Friends, be at peace. Families, be at peace with one another. Beloved of God, be at peace in your hearts, in your souls, and in your minds. Offer one another a sign of God's peace with the words: "Peace be with you." May these be God's word on our lips and in our hearts.

Response to the Word (Genesis 37, Psalm 105, Matthew 14)
   Brothers betray brothers,
      yet God remains faithful.
   Families turn their backs on their own,
      yet God remains true.
   Believers sink in the waters of fear and doubt,
      yet God remains our firm foundation.
   When all other help vanishes,
      God remains. Thanks be to God.
   (B. J. Beu)

THANKSGIVING AND COMMUNION

Offering Prayer (Genesis 37, Psalm 105)
   Through our struggles, you carve out hope.
   Through our suffering, you give us gifts—
      gifts not just for us, but to give away.
   Gracious, almighty God,
      receive the fruit of our struggles
         and the pain of our suffering.
   Receive our lives, our whole lives,
      and every step on our journeys,
         that we might shine with your glory
            in all our endeavors. Amen.

Introduction to Communion (Romans 10)
> Glory to God in the highest,
> > **peace to all people on earth.**
> We praise you, bless you, and adore you.
> > **We give you thanks for your great goodness.**
> Lord Jesus Christ, Lamb of God, Son of the Father,
> you take away the sin of the world.
> > **Have mercy on us.**
> We love you and we trust you, with the Holy Spirit,
> > **to manifest your great purposes.**
> With the people of God in every place and time,
> we praise you:
> > **Holy, holy, holy Lord, God of power and might,**
> > > **heaven and earth are full of your glory.**
> > **Hosanna in the highest.**
> Do not be anxious about God's salvation.
> It matters not how good you are
> > or how happy you are.
> It matters not how big your faith is
> > or how loud your voice echoes.
> If your heart is open to God,
> > you are in God.
> If your mouth is open to speak truth,
> > you are in God.
> I invite you now to confess your faith:
> > **I confess with my lips that Jesus is Lord.**
> > **I believe in my heart**
> > > **that God raised him from the dead.**
> Friends, you are saved; you are put right with God.
> Be at peace. Be confident. You are a friend of God.
> In Christ there are no divisions, no distinctions.
> Christ is the same friend to all, the Lord of all.
> Everyone who calls on the name of the Lord
> > will be saved.

We stand now, as friends around this open table,
    in this act of communion.
Together, we are members of Christ, one with God,
    fed by God, nourished by the Spirit.
Holy Spirit, you gather us up in faith
    and give us confidence of our salvation.
Be present in us and between us.
Be present in this bread and this wine,
    that it may be for us the body and blood
       of our Lord, Jesus Christ. Amen.
Friends of God, come and share.
Body of Christ, take and eat.

Communion Prayer (Romans 10)

As we have been fed,
    so God sends us to feed others.
As we have received good news,
    so God sends us out to be good news.
For how can others hear unless we speak?
And how can we speak unless we are sent?
Go and share the news of God's great love,
    for lovely are the feet of those
       who bring good news!

SENDING FORTH

Benediction (Genesis 37, Matthew 14)

May the God of the journey walk with you—
    in and out of pits, and in and out of storms.
May our Creator God continue to form you
    and bless you.
May the God of grace encourage you,
    this day, and every day, and beyond our days.
Amen.

ADDITIONAL RESOURCES

Time with the Children (Genesis 37, Matthew 14)

Both the "Joseph in the pit" and the "Peter sinking" stories have huge potential to engage children. Choose one; don't attempt both!

With Joseph, every child can relate to feeling rejected, and many can relate to feeling bullied. Use the architecture of your church to create a "pit" (e.g., pretend to push someone off a step). Talk about bullying and how we use harsh words (or worse) to push people away. Try to understand what motivated the brothers, and what ethical principles kept them from further violence.

See the psalm of hope, below, for a liturgy about bullying.

With Peter, create a "boat" that the children can stand on (e.g., a pew) and some "lake" (e.g., with a tarpaulin or large fabric piece). Congregation members can hold the edges of the fabric while children try to "walk on the water." Discuss fears and trying to be brave.

Liturgy of Hope (Psalm 27)

My God is my light.
My God is my savior.
Why be afraid?
My God is my safety.
My God is my home.
I won't be afraid!
I might get teased.
I might get hurt.
But I don't need to be scared.
People may call me names and try to bully me,
        but I will stand tall!

With God's care around me,
    I will sing and dance and shout for joy!
With God's face shining on me,
    I will be patient through bad days.
I will be strong.
Take courage, my heart,
    and lean on God.

August 20, 2023

Twelfth Sunday after Pentecost
Proper 15

Paula A. Ferris

[handwritten: 104 O Worship the King; 139 Great is Thy Faithfulness]

COLOR
Green

SCRIPTURE READINGS

Genesis 45:1-15; Psalm 133; Romans 11:1-2a, 29-32;
Matthew 15:(10-20) 21-28

THEME IDEAS

The relationship between "inside" and "outside," what
defiles and what heals, is in high relief in the Matthew
passage. Jesus speaks to the contrast between outward
cleanliness and soul cleanliness. And he speaks to
an "outsider" in the Canaanite women. In Jesus, God
speaks with a human voice, reminding us that insiders
and outsiders and all kinds of prayers belong in the circle of God's grace and love.

INVITATION AND GATHERING

Centering Words (Psalm 133)
How good it is that sisters and brothers live together in
human dignity. As we celebrate our common humanity

this day, let us lift up a humane spirituality in song and
silence, prayer and practice.

Call to Worship (Matthew 15)
> Every sense is bombarded daily
> with the sound of hurtful words
> and the touch of polluted air and water.
> > **God's Spirit cleanses us**
> > **with every breath we take**
> > **as we breathe out our praise.**
> Every sense is bombarded daily,
> with the taste of food that does not satisfy
> and the whiff of corruption.
> > **God's Spirit cleanses us**
> > **with every breath we take**
> > **as we breathe out our praise.**
> Every sense is bombarded daily
> with sights that disturb and distract.
> > **God's Spirit cleanses us**
> > **with every breath we take**
> > **as we breathe out our praise.**
> Let us praise our maker while we have breath.

Opening Prayer (Matthew 15)
> We cry to you, O Lord,
> > from the back of the line,
> > from the edge of the crowd,
> > from the corner of the room.
> But you make no such distinctions,
> > nor do you set such boundaries.
> Your faithfulness is great;
> > your grace is enough.
> And we are covered in your love.

–OR–

Opening Prayer (Genesis 45, Psalm 133, Romans 11, Matthew 15)
> Eternal God,
>> part the veil that blinds us to our unity.
> When our families hurt and betray us,
>> help us find ways to let go of our pain
>>> and work for the healing of all people.
> When we feel abandoned by those we love,
>> help us trust in the power of forgiveness
>>> and seek to bring peace and reconciliation.
> When our hearts are pierced with anguish,
>> help us reach out to those who can bring us solace
>>> and find in the search, grace upon grace,
>>>> through your loving Spirit. Amen.
> *(B. J. Beu)*

PROCLAMATION AND RESPONSE

Prayer of Confession (Genesis 45, Matthew 15)
> God of grace, you invite us to draw near
>> and embrace the circle of your love.
> We come in anguish at our broken relationships—
>> our alienation from one another,
>> our resistance to reconciliation,
>> our readiness to be the blind following the blind,
>> and our readiness to give up
>>> when persistence is called for.
> Gather us in, and make a place to heal our anguish,
>> ease our alienation, and end our resistance.
> Ready us for reconciliation, forbearance, and persistence.
> Turn our gaze to the one who calls our name.

Words of Assurance (Genesis 45, Matthew 15)
    In coming forth, we take a single step,
        and God faithfully bridges the gap.
    You are loved and your spirit is healed
        in the embrace of a God of love and healing.

Introduction to the Word (Matthew 15, Genesis 45)
    The Canaanite woman cries out,
        claiming God's grace.
    Joseph reaches out to his brothers in tears,
        claiming grace for them all.
    Resistance melts when what is right in God's kin-dom
        emerges in a flood of tears and a wave of grace.

Response to the Word (Genesis 45, Psalm 133, Romans 11, Matthew 15)
    Even in the midst of tragedy and loss,
    God is at work, preserving a remnant.
    Even in the midst of insult and injury,
    God is at work, healing the needy.
    Even in the midst of abandonment and rejection,
    God is at work, saving the faithful.
    God challenges us to look beyond our differences
    and embrace what we have in common.
    God's grace unites us in a fellowship of love.
    Thanks be to God!
    (B. J. Beu)

THANKSGIVING AND COMMUNION

Invitation to the Offering (Matthew 15)
    As we learn to live generously, what we take in ceases to poison us and what goes out heals the world. As we learn to live generously, we restore human dignity to the center of our faith.

Offering Prayer (Genesis 45)
Bountiful God, you are the source of all good things.
When famine threatened the world,
  you blessed Joseph with dreams
    to preserve life and save people far and wide.
When hunger threatens our world,
  you bless us with dreams
    to preserve life and prevent disaster.
When our dreams are your dreams, Gracious God,
  the world is truly blessed.
Accept these gifts,
  as a pledge to work and live your dream
    that all may live together in unity. Amen.

SENDING FORTH

Benediction (Genesis 45, Psalm 133, Romans 11, Matthew 15)
Come out from the back of the line.
Come out from the edge of the crowd.
Come out from the corner of the room.
Embrace others and be embraced—
  that the least, the last, and the lost
  may come out of the shadows
  and live in the light.
Embrace the world and be embraced.

August 27, 2023

Thirteenth Sunday after Pentecost
Proper 16

Mary Scifres
Copyright © Mary Scifres

342 *Rock of Ages*

COLOR
Green   686 *O God Our Help in Ages Past*

SCRIPTURE READINGS

Exodus 1:8–2:10; Psalm 124; Romans 12:1-8;
Matthew 16:13-20

THEME IDEAS

Paul invites us to present our bodies as a living sacrifice to God, dedicating ourselves so fully that God
can transform us by renewing our minds and revealing
God's will. The great stories of our faith are filled with
moments of ordinary people doing just this. Exodus reveals midwives risking their lives to save the Hebrew
children. Pharaoh's daughter recognizes a refugee
child and saves him from the water. And Moses's sister
stands watch to protect her brother and re-unite him
with his mother. Peter proclaims Jesus as the Christ,
and Jesus proclaims Peter as the rock upon whom God

will build the church. Whether we are mighty or small, God is not only our helper but also our maker. Having created us in the divine image, God invites us to give ourselves fully. In so doing, we open the door for God to transform our lives, and through us, to transform the world.

INVITATION AND GATHERING

Centering Words (Exodus 2, Romans 12)
When we give ourselves fully to God, God transforms our lives. In this transformation, God connects us to others whose lives are being transformed, as they too give themselves fully to God.

Call to Worship (Psalm 124, Romans 12)
Our help is in God,
who calls us to worship.
Our hope is in love,
that calls us to care.
Come, let us bring our full selves to worship.
Let us bring our full love and care.

Opening Prayer (Romans 12)
Gracious and loving God, bless us with your presence
as we worship this day.
Bless us with your love
as we grow in love and mature faith.
Bless us with your guidance
as we give ourselves to you, to your church,
and to your work in the world. Amen.

PROCLAMATION AND RESPONSE

Prayer of Yearning (Exodus 2, Psalm 124, Romans 12, Matthew 16)
> Rock of ages, be our fortress and our shelter
> in troubled times.
> Be our strength and our courage when we are afraid.
> Be our grace and our forgiveness when we fall short.
> Be our inspiration and our guide
> when we strive to serve you and your world fully.
> In hope and gratitude, we pray. Amen.

Words of Assurance (Psalm 124)
> Our help is in God, the maker of heaven and earth.
> God is our rock, a fortress of mercy and grace.

Passing the Peace of Christ (Romans 12)
> We are the body of Christ, a community of differing gifts. Each of us is called to give ourselves fully to God and to one another. As we share signs of peace today, remember our connection in call and service to lift and encourage one another.

Introduction to the Word (Romans 12)
> As we listen for God's still-speaking voice, may the words we hear, the thoughts we think, and the wisdom we glean transform our lives by the renewing of our minds and the maturing of our faith.

Response to the Word (Romans 12)
> We are the body of Christ.
> **We each have gifts to share.**
> We are the people of God.
> **We all have ways to serve.**
> We are a community of faith.
> **We are one in generous sacrifice and love.**

THANKSGIVING AND COMMUNION

Invitation to the Offering (Romans 12)
Sisters and brothers, as Paul encouraged the earliest
Christians, I invite you now to present yourselves and
your gifts as a living sacrifice, holy and pleasing to God.

Offering Prayer (Romans 12)
Ever-giving God, help us give as fully
to you and to your world
as you have given to us.
Transform our gifts with your love,
that they may become vessels
of your love for others.
Amen.

SENDING FORTH

Benediction (Romans 12)
My friends, we are the body of Christ,
built on the foundation of God's grace.
Go now to love and serve
in your unique and individual ways.
As people connected in call and in love,
give yourselves fully to God and God's world.

September 3, 2023

Fourteenth Sunday after Pentecost
Proper 17

B. J. Beu
Copyright © B. J. Beu

3 Holy Holy Holy
596 I Surrender All

COLOR

Green

SCRIPTURE READINGS

Exodus 3:1-15; Psalm 105:1-6, 23-26, 45b;
Romans 12:9-21; Matthew 16:21-28

THEME IDEAS

Knowing when to turn aside makes all the difference
in the world. Moses sees a burning bush and turns
aside to see what is afoot. Only then does God call to
Moses from the fire. The psalmist urges the people to
turn aside from everyday cares to seek the Lord—the
source of strength and miracles, the fountain of wonder and joy. Paul exhorts the church of Rome to forsake
feelings of resentment and hate, but instead repay evil
with good, doing what is noble in the sight of all. Jesus
rebukes Peter for succumbing to worldly considerations
over God's purposes. To find our lives, we must lose

them. Such turning leads us to realize we are standing
on holy ground.

INVITATION AND GATHERING

Centering Words (Exodus 3)
God speaks from burning bushes and souls on fire. May
God grant us eyes to see and ears to hear, as we worship
this day.

Call to Worship (Exodus 3, Psalm 105)
Give thanks to the Lord.
Call on God's holy name.
Sing praises to the Lord.
Tell of God's wondrous deeds.
Let the faithful sing of the Lord's awesome power.
Let the hearts of the faithful rejoice.
Give thanks to the Lord.
Call on God's holy name.

Opening Prayer (Exodus 3, Romans 12)
Great I Am, you come to us in unexpected ways.
Excite our curiosity,
that we might turn aside
and realize we are standing on holy ground.
Appear to us in fire and wonder,
that we might see worlds
beyond the reaches of our imaginations.
Reveal the glory of your kingdom—
where love is genuine,
where evil is forsaken,
where mutual affection abides,
and hospitality is shown to strangers,
where all are made one. Amen.

PROCLAMATION AND RESPONSE

Prayer of Yearning (Exodus 3, Romans 12)
> Loving God, Holy Shepherd,
>   we long for a higher calling.
> When we would rather tend our flocks in peace
>   than confront the powers of this age,
>   open our hearts to your guidance and direction.
> When we would rather keep silent
>   than face the suffering of others,
>   open our mouths to speak your truth.
> Turn us from human considerations
>   and set our minds on your kingdom,
>   through Christ, our Lord. Amen.

Words of Assurance (Exodus 3, Psalm 105)
> The great I Am invites us to turn aside
>   and boldly embrace paths that lead to life.
> Turn and receive blessing upon blessing.

Passing the Peace of Christ (Romans 12)
> The Prince of Peace leads us into life. With this hope and this promise, turn to one another and pass the peace of Christ.

Introduction to the Word (Exodus 3)
> As we listen for the word of God, turn aside from the worries and cares that imprison us in cages of our own making. Listen with awe and wonder to the great I Am—the one who invites us to new and wondrous possibilities. Listen well, for we worship on holy ground.

Response to the Word (Romans 12)
> Live peaceably with all.
> Hold fast to what is good.
> Honor what is just and show mutual affection for all.
> Do this and you will live.

THANKSGIVING AND COMMUNION

Offering Prayer (Romans 12)
>God of new beginnings, receive the gifts of our hands,
>>that hospitality might be extended to those in need.
>Bless today's offering,
>>that the hungry may be fed
>>>and the thirsty may be satisfied.
>May these gifts seal our commitment
>>to do what is just and honorable in your sight.
>Amen.

SENDING FORTH

Benediction (Romans 12)
>Live peaceably with others.
>Hold fast to what is good.
>Honor what is just
>>and show mutual affection for all.
>Go with the blessings of the almighty.

September 10, 2023

Fifteenth Sunday after Pentecost
Proper 18

Michael Beu
Copyright © Michael Beu

COLOR

Green

[handwritten: 104 O Worship the King]
[handwritten: 139 Great is Thy Faithfulness]

SCRIPTURE READINGS

Exodus 12:1-14; Psalm 149; Romans 13:8-14;
Matthew 18:15-20

THEME IDEAS

God's love protected the Israelites as death passed over
them. God's love preserves our lives with hope and new
possibilities for the future. Paul reminds us that love is
the true fulfillment of God's law, and that the love of
God allows us to love freely and abundantly. Because of
God's love for us, human reconciliation and forgiveness
are possible. Sing for joy, for God's love is a steadfast
and faithful presence in our lives.

INVITATION AND GATHERING

Centering Words (Exodus 12)
Place your hope and trust in the Lord, whose faithful
love watches over your homes in times of greatest need.

Call to Worship (Psalm 149)
Sing a new song to God.
Sing of light and hope.
Dance with laughter and joy.
Dance with hearts full of love.
Rejoice with strings and drums.
Rejoice with justice and peace.
Sing a new song to God.

Opening Prayer (Exodus 12, Romans 13, Matthew 18)
Ancient of days, we enter your presence
    to remember and rejoice.
We come looking for your steadfast faithfulness
    and your loving care.
May we be a people who seek reconciliation
    and genuine forgiveness with one another.
In remembrance and gratitude for your mercy
    and your grace, we pray. Amen.

PROCLAMATION AND RESPONSE

Prayer of Yearning (Exodus 12, Romans 13, Matthew 18)
Gracious God, amidst our songs of joy,
    our hearts are touched by fear.
Sin plagues our world,
    even as we strive to build your realm.

Sorrow enters our lives,
    even as we put on false smiles
        and engage in empty conversations.
Death lurks around every corner,
    even as we struggle against our own mortality.
Reconcile us with your love and compassion,
    and bless us with your compassionate presence,
        that we may be filled with joy, love,
            and hope this day. Amen.

Words of Assurance (Romans 13, Matthew 18)
    Wherever two or three are gathered in Christ's name,
        God is with us.
    Where God is, grace and compassion abide.
    In the grace of God and the love of Christ,
        we are made one in ministry to the world.

Passing the Peace of Christ (Matthew 18)
    Set aside sorrow and past resentments. Embrace Christ's
    gift of healing and reconciliation as we share signs of
    peace with one another.

Response to the Word or Benediction (Romans 13)
    Now's the time . . .
        Time to wake from sleep.
    Time to set aside the hurts of the past.
        Time to see Christ's shining hope.
    Time to embrace God's glorious wisdom.
        Time to put on love as the clothing of life.
    Now's the time . . .
        Time to live as the people of God.

THANKSGIVING AND COMMUNION

Invitation to the Offering (Exodus 12, Romans 13)
In Christ, all gifts are welcome, both great and small.
Bathed in love, led by compassion, let us share our gifts
and offerings with God.

Offering Prayer (Romans 13)
Receive these gifts as offerings of love, O God.
Bless them with your grace,
that those who receive them
may find compassion and hope.
In your holy name, we pray. Amen.

SENDING FORTH

Benediction (Exodus 12, Matthew 18)
Just as God has called us here,
God now sends us forth.
Just as God has joined us here,
God goes with us now.
Go with the power of God
to love and serve the world.

September 17, 2023

Sixteenth Sunday after Pentecost
Proper 19

Rebecca J. Kruger Gaudino

COLOR
Green

185 Jesus Loves Me
92 O How I Love Jesus

SCRIPTURE READINGS

Exodus 14:19-31; Exodus 15:1b-11, 20-21;
Romans 14:1-12; Matthew 18:21-35

THEME IDEAS

The story of the Egyptian army's total destruction can be hard to read. And yet, this story has been incredibly important for all who experience oppression and yearn for God's liberation. The dead bodies and wrecked chariots on the shores of the Red Sea communicate God's rejection of oppression, as Miriam and the women celebrate with song and dance. The Talmud records that God stops the angels from singing their praise, for how can they rejoice when God's creatures are drowning? Perhaps these are the two responses we need to hold together: celebration that evil is conquered and the realization that this triumph means suffering for others. In Romans, Paul addresses issues that undermine the church—how we diminish one another and the church. How do we live God's righteous initiatives while remembering the humanity of our adversaries?

INVITATION AND GATHERING

Centering Words (Exodus 15, Romans 14)
O God, you are our strength and our salvation.
You uphold and save us. We offer you our very lives.

Call to Worship (Exodus 14, Exodus 15, Romans 14)
Sing to God, for God has triumphed gloriously!
God is our strength and our might!
Long ago God freed the slaves from Egypt,
opening passage through the Red Sea waters.
Here and now, God is our salvation,
leading us through dangerous waters.
Who is like our God, majestic in holiness
and awesome in splendor?
Every knee shall bow, every voice shall praise
the God of wonder.

Opening Prayer (Exodus 15, Romans 14)
We sing to you, O God, for you have been our strength.
You open the waters of suffering
    and lead us safely through.
You uphold us in times of deep distress
    and we exalt your holy name.
Receive our honor and thanks, mighty God. Amen.

PROCLAMATION AND RESPONSE

Prayer of Yearning (Exodus 14, Exodus 15, Romans 14)
When we hear praises of your past help and triumph,
    we wonder where you are today, O God.

We look at our lives
and see hurtful relationships.
We look at our nation
and see communities suffering under oppression.
We look at our world
and see injustice and brutality.
We need your mighty arm
to shatter wrongdoing and corruption.
When we are weak,
strengthen our faith.
When we despair,
renew our hope.
When we give up,
stand us up in your just cause,
that we might live for you. Amen.

Words of Assurance (Romans 14)
We stand before God—a God of justice,
a God of forgiveness and acceptance.
This God raises us up and upholds us in our living.
Praise be to God!

Passing the Peace of Christ (Romans 14)
As we stand before God, accepted and upheld, let us
greet one another as brothers and sisters in this gathered
community.

Introduction to the Word (Exodus 14, Exodus 15)
Today we hear a familiar story. Hear it with new ears!
Let it shock you. Let it move you. Would *you* dance and
play *your* tambourine? Listen to this amazing story of an
impossible getaway made possible by God.

*Response to the Word/Litany (Exodus 14, Exodus 15,
Romans 14)*
Give us eyes to see the suffering of our world, O God,
that we may clearly see those who are wounded
and those who wound.

Help us feel, in the very core of our being,
    your yearning to bring wholeness to all.
Make us healers in your service. Amen.

THANKSGIVING AND COMMUNION

Invitation to the Offering (Exodus 14, Exodus 15,
Romans 14)
    Let us share gifts of every kind in the service of God's
    healing justice and love.

Offering Prayer (Exodus 14, Exodus 15, Romans 14)
    Savior God, you look at our world with compassion.
    You also look at our world with clarity
        and a zeal for justice.
    Use all we bring to life, and all we bring to you today,
        to fight for justice with mercy and compassion.
    Make us and our gifts part of the healing of the world.
    Amen.

SENDING FORTH

Benediction (Exodus 14, Exodus 15, Romans 14)
    Who is like our majestic God?
    The One who is wonder-worker
    and awesome in splendor.
        No other!
    God calls to us to join the holy work
    of making the world right.
        We will live for God and for God's world
        in all we do. Amen.

September 24, 2023

Seventeenth Sunday after Pentecost
Proper 20

B. J. Beu
Copyright © B. J. Beu

[handwritten notes: 692, 138, God Will Take Care of You, I Need Thee Every Hour]

COLOR

Green

SCRIPTURE READINGS

Exodus 16:2-15; Psalm 105:1-6, 37-45; Philippians 1:21-30; Matthew 20:1-16

THEME IDEAS

Although God provides everything we need to live, we find things to complain about. In Exodus, the congregation complains of hunger and how life was better back in Egypt. The psalmist extols God's bountiful response to the people's wilderness complaining: providing quail in the evening, bread of heaven in the morning, and water from a rock. Paul complains about having to remain here on earth, when he could be with Christ in heaven. In Matthew, the day laborers complain they are treated unfairly for being paid the same wages as those who worked only a short time. Yet, God will be God, showering blessings with equity, even when we complain; perhaps, especially when we complain. And this, while frequently vexing, is good news.

INVITATION AND GATHERING

Centering Words (Exodus 16, Psalm 105, Matthew 20)
God showers us with blessings, even when we complain. Perhaps especially when we complain. This is good news indeed!

Call to Worship (Psalm 105, Matthew 20)
Give thanks to the Lord.
Call on God's holy name.
Sing praises to our God.
Tell of God's wonderful works.
The Lord offers bread from heaven
to satisfy our hunger.
God issues water from solid rock
to quench our thirst.
Give thanks to the Lord.
Let everything that draws breath praise God.

Opening Prayer (Exodus 16, Psalm 105)
Guide our way, Caretaker God,
in the wilderness of our lives.
Offer us the bread of heaven,
that we may taste your Spirit
and be nourished in body and soul.
Reveal your presence among us
and show us the tender mercies of your love.
In joy and jubilation, we pray. Amen.

PROCLAMATION AND RESPONSE

Prayer of Yearning (Exodus 16, Psalm 105, Matthew 20)
> God of infinite patience, we turn complaining
>> into an Olympic sport:
>> "The journey is too long.
>> The road is hard and our feet hurt.
>> We're hungry and bored.
>> This isn't what we signed up for!"
> You've heard it all before, faithful One.
> You'll hear it all again.
> Yet, you never forsake us in our grumbling.
> Shower us with your manifold blessings
>> and open our lips to sing songs of gratitude.
> For we are weary of our complaining
>> and long to make a fresh start. Amen.

Words of Assurance (Psalm 105)
> Rejoice, you who seek the Lord.
> Count your blessings, not your troubles.
> For in acts of gratitude, you will find peace.

Passing the Peace of Christ (Matthew 20)
> The first shall be last and the last shall be first. In holy wisdom, let us seek the peace and welfare of one another as we share signs of Christ's peace.

Response to the Word (Psalm 105, Philippians 1, Matthew 20)
> Gratitude is worthy of the gospel.
>> **We will give thanks for our food and drink.**
> Love is worthy of the gospel.
>> **We will share the love of God**
>> **and the peace of Christ.**

Offer blessings that are worthy of the gospel.
**We will offer the Spirit's blessings
in everything we say and in everything we do.**

THANKSGIVING AND COMMUNION

Invitation to the Offering (Psalm 105)
In the wilderness of our lives, God's grace is like water flowing from a rock, transforming arid desert into flowing rivers. In thanksgiving for God's mercy, let us give from our abundance as we collect today's offering.

Offering Prayer (Exodus 16, Philippians 1, Matthew 20)
Gracious God, you provide bread in the wilderness
and life-giving waters in the desert.
We offer you our thanks and praise.
May our gifts and offerings bless your world—
that all may be blessed,
and all may find purpose and passion,
through Christ, our Lord. Amen.

SENDING FORTH

Benediction (Exodus 16, Matthew 20)
God meets us on our wilderness journeys,
that we may not journey alone.
Christ tends us on our wilderness journeys,
that we may receive our daily bread.
The Spirit sustains on our wilderness journeys,
that we may be strengthened for what lies ahead.
Go with God's blessings.

October 1, 2023

Eighteenth Sunday after Pentecost
Proper 21
World Communion Sunday

Mary Scifres
Copyright © Mary Scifres

[handwritten: Ps 11]

COLOR

Green

[handwritten: 630 What A Friend]
[handwritten: 434 Revive Us Again]

SCRIPTURE READINGS

Exodus 17:1-7; Psalm 78:1-4, 12-16; Philippians 2:1-13;
Matthew 21:23-32

THEME IDEAS

On World Communion Sunday, the scriptures from Exodus and Matthew vividly display how challenging reconciliation and unity can be, particularly when we thirst and hunger for things that have not yet arrived. Even so, God's glory is in our midst, inviting us to recognize God's presence and authority, and to claim reconciliation and unity. Only then can we have the things for which we hunger and thirst: peace and justice, mercy and compassion among others. This is the very unity the Philippians passage calls us to achieve, particularly on World Communion Sunday: Be of one mind, the mind of Christ.

INVITATION AND GATHERING

Centering Words (Philippians 2)

Be of one mind, the mind of Christ. Be of one Spirit, the Spirit of God's love. Be of one purpose as beloved people of God.

Call to Worship (Exodus 17, Philippians 2)

The God of glory awaits,
   welcoming us to worship and praise.
The Christ of humility is here,
   welcoming our needs and prayers.
The Spirit of love gathers us in,
   binding us together as one.

Opening Prayer (Philippians 2)

God of wondrous love and glorious deeds,
   shower us with your love
      and quench our thirst for grace.
Strengthen us with your Spirit of power
   and embolden us to live our faith.
Humble us with the example of Christ
   and remind us to regard one another
      as beloved children of God. Amen.

PROCLAMATION AND RESPONSE

Prayer of Confession (Exodus 17, Philippians 2)

Prince of peace, speak mercy amidst our quarrels
   and our dissensions.

Shower us with your love,
    that we may remember to love others
        as fully as you love us.
Bind us together with your Spirit,
    that we might live as one people—
        a people of one mind, one love,
            and one all-embracing compassion for all.

Words of Assurance (Philippians 2)
    Christ is at work within you,
        filling you with mercy and grace.
    Christ enables you to work for God's good pleasure.

Passing the Peace of Christ (Philippians 2)
    Let us share signs of encouragement, compassion, consolation, and love, as we pass the peace of Christ.

Introduction to the Word (Psalm 78, Matthew 21)
    Give ear to hear the teachings of Christ.
    Listen to God's glorious deeds
        and reflect on the wonders of God's love.

Response to the Word (Exodus 17, Philippians 2, Matthew 21)
    What is the mind of Christ?
        To love and serve.
    What is the mind of Christ?
        To work in God's world.
    What is the mind of Christ?
        To be humble and kind.
    What is the mind of Christ?
        To be compassionate and peaceful.
    May this mind be in us.
        May it define our speaking and our acting.
    May it guide our coming and our going,
        our living and our dying. Amen.

THANKSGIVING AND COMMUNION

Offering Prayer (Philippians 2)
Beloved and loving God, bless these gifts,
that they may bring unity to a world in strife.
Bless our lives,
that we may bring love to everyone we meet.
Bless our church,
that our fellowship may be a place of unity
and inclusion for all. Amen.

Invitation to Communion (Philippians 2)
This is the table of unity and love.
This is the table of mercy and grace.
All are welcome; be of one mind and one heart.
We come with joy, with the mind of love.
Come, all things are ready.
And all are welcome here.

The Great Thanksgiving (Philippians 2)
God be with you.
And also with you.
Lift up your hearts.
We lift them up to God.
Let us give thanks to the God of unity and love.
It is right to give our thanks and praise.
It is right and a good and joyful thing,
always and everywhere, to give thanks to you,
almighty God, creator of heaven and earth.
In the beginning, you created us from dust.
You called us to live in your image
and to be of one mind.
Even when we grumbled and complained,
and we argued and fought,
you called us to unity and love.

Even when we neglected your teachings
   and turned away from your call,
   you invited us back into your vineyard
   of mercy and grace.
And so, with your people on earth
   and all the company of heaven,
   we praise your name and join their unending hymn:
   Holy, holy, holy One, God of power and might,
   heaven and earth are full of your glory.
   Hosanna in the highest. Blessed is the one
   who comes in the name of God.
   Hosanna in the highest.
Holy are you and blessed is your beloved name.
In the fullness of time, you sent Christ Jesus
   to call us anew to abundant life, compassionate love,
   and unity with you and your people.
With encouragement and grace, Christ calls us now
   to join in unity with his followers around the world.
May we be of one mind, live as one people,
   and love with the power of your grace.
Through this amazing grace,
   we are invited to your table,
   welcomed in your love,
   and reclaimed as sisters and brothers of Christ.
As children of your mercy and grace,
   we come with humble hearts and open minds,
   remembering how Jesus shared a feast of love,
   and how he invites us even now
   to share this feast of love with one another.
On that night before his death, Jesus took bread,
   gave thanks to you, broke the bread,
   gave it to the disciples, saying:
   "Take, eat; this is my body which is given for you.
   Do this in remembrance of me."

When the supper was over, Jesus took the cup,
    gave thanks to you,
    and gave it to the disciples, saying:
    "Drink from this, all of you;
    this is my life in the new covenant,
    poured out for you and for many
    for the forgiveness of sins.
    Do this, as often as you drink it,
    in remembrance of me."
And so, in remembrance of these,
    your life-giving acts of love and grace,
    we offer ourselves in praise and thanksgiving
    as children of your love,
    in union with Christ's love for us,
    and our love for one another,
    as we proclaim the mystery of faith.
    Christ has died.
    Christ is risen.
    Christ will come again.

Communion Prayer (Philippians 2)
    Pour out your Holy Spirit on us
        and on these gifts of bread and wine.
    Make them be for us the life and love of Christ,
        that we may be the body of Christ for the world,
            redeemed and unified by Christ's love and grace.
    By your Spirit, make us one with Christ,
        one with one another,
            and one in ministry to all the world,
                until Christ comes in final victory
                    and we feast at your heavenly banquet.
    Through Jesus Christ,
        with the Holy Spirit in your holy church,
            all honor and glory is yours, almighty God,
                now and forevermore. Amen.

Giving the Bread and Cup
(The bread and wine are given to the people with these or other words of blessing.)

The body of Christ, calling us to be children of God.
The love of Christ, calling us to love as we are loved.

SENDING FORTH

Benediction (Philippians 2)
Share the Spirit.
Encourage others in Christ.
Go forth to give God's love and encouragement
to the world.

October 8, 2023

Nineteenth Sunday after Pentecost
Proper 22

Mary Scifres
Copyright © Mary Scifres

Isa 61:1,2
Luke 4:16-21

563 Open My Eyes that I May See

548

COLOR

Green

SCRIPTURE READINGS

Exodus 20:1-4, 7-9, 12-20; Psalm 19; Philippians 3:4b-14;
Matthew 21:33-46

THEME IDEAS

The mysteries of God reveal themselves in so many
ways: commandments given on tablets of stone, teachings told through poetry and the oral stories of God's
people through the ages, the testimony of pressing toward a heavenly goal, and even a Messiah who predict-
ed the world's rejection and his own eventual death. In
these scriptures, mysteries emerge—each slightly different—but each with lessons to teach.

INVITATION AND GATHERING

Centering Words (Exodus 20, Psalm 19, Matthew 21)
In the scriptures found in the Bible, you will find commandments of old and lessons from enigmatic parables. But there is an older scripture—a scripture beyond words, a scripture as deep and mysterious as the night sky. For the heavens proclaim God's glory with every colorful sunrise and budding flower.

Call to Worship (Psalm 19, Matthew 21)
Christ the cornerstone welcomes us to this house of God.
May our minds perceive God's word,
even as our hearts receive God's love.
May God's Spirit bless us with wisdom and faith.

Opening Prayer (Psalm 19, Philippians 3)
Holy Spirit, heavenly God, shine upon us
with the wisdom of ancient words.
Enlighten our minds,
that we may perceive your presence.
Strengthen our resolve,
that we may press toward growth
in love and faith.
Help us grow closer to your likeness
each and every day. Amen.

PROCLAMATION AND RESPONSE

Prayer of Confession (Psalm 19, Philippians 3, Matthew 21)
God of grace and God of glory,
bless us with your mercy
and your steadfast love.

When we pursue pointless gains
and embark on dead-end journeys,
guide us back to your ways.
When we strive for our own righteousness,
remind us that your righteousness is all we need.
When we reject your teaching,
or, even worse, reject your presence,
love us and correct our ways.
Forgive us and welcome us home
into the arms of your grace and love. Amen.

Words of Assurance (Exodus 20, Philippians 3)
Do not be afraid, God's love is strong enough
to overcome our weaknesses.

Introduction to the Word (Psalm 19, Philippians 3)
May the words of our mouths be acceptable to God
and be blessings to the world.
May the meditations of our hearts,
and the reflections of our minds,
bring us closer to God and to God's love.
May the beauty of God's creation
bring us closer to God's teachings
and to a knowledge of how to love God's world.

Response to the Word (Psalm 19, Philippians 3)
O God, our rock and our redeemer,
be our strong foundation,
even when we are unsteady.
Be our guiding light,
even when we wander in darkness.
Be our steadfast faithfulness,
even when our faith falters.
Be our coach and our cheerleader,
and push us to grow closer to you, closer to love,
and closer to your creation. Amen.

THANKSGIVING AND COMMUNION

Offering Prayer (Psalm 19)
>Blessed One, bless those who receive these gifts.
>Bless our words, our actions, and our gifts,
>>that they may be blessings for your world.
>And bless these offerings and this time of worship,
>>even as you strengthen this community of faith
>>and the ministries of this church. Amen.

SENDING FORTH

Benediction (Psalm 19, Philippians 3, Matthew 5)
>You are the light of the world!
>>**We will shine with love**
>>**as the stars shine with glory.**
>You are the light of the world!
>>**We will reveal God's brilliance**
>>**in word and deed.**
>As we move forward to what lies ahead,
>>**we will press on toward the goal of love.**

October 15, 2023

Twentieth Sunday after Pentecost
Proper 23

B. J. Beu
Copyright © B. J. Beu

[handwritten notes: Lev 19:17,18; Lu 10:25-37; 648 Love Divine; 654 Take Time to be Holy]

COLOR

Green

SCRIPTURE READINGS

Exodus 32:1-14; Psalm 106:1-6, 19-23; Philippians 4:1-9;
Matthew 22:1-14

THEME IDEAS

We are to praise God and rejoice in the Lord always. The early Israelites knew this, but they decided to fashion new gods for themselves when Moses took so long coming down from the mountain of God. The psalmist exhorts the people to praise the Lord because God is good. God's faithful love endures forever. Philippians exhorts the people to rejoice in God and be glad, focusing our thoughts and attentions on the things in this world that are good and honorable and just. Matthew's Gospel recounts a baffling tale of a king burning down the city of those who refuse to come to a royal wedding. The king then invites those on the highways and byways, only to toss out a conscripted guest for lacking proper wedding clothes. Unless you want to argue that the clothing is metaphorical for the virtues in Philippians, this passage stands alone.

INVITATION AND GATHERING

Centering Words (Psalm 106, Philippians 4)
Rejoice in the Lord always. God is worthy of our hearts' delight.

Call to Worship (Philippians 4)
Rejoice in God always. Again I say, Rejoice!
Take heart; the Lord is near.
Make it known among the people: God reigns.
Proclaim it from the rooftops.
Let gentleness and mirth be your guide.
Rejoice in God always. Again I say, Rejoice!
Take heart; the Lord is near.

Opening Prayer (Psalm 106, Philippians 4)
Holy God, we come before you this day
    with praise on our lips
        and songs of joy in our hearts.
When we abide in your kingdom
    and live according to your ways,
        good triumphs over evil,
        love is stronger than hate,
            and truth wins the day.
Focus our hearts and minds
    on things that are worthy of praise,
        and bless us with a peace
            that passes all understanding. Amen.

PROCLAMATION AND RESPONSE

Prayer of Yearning (Psalm 106, Philippians 4)
We seek your goodness, O God,
for we search our hearts and find them wanting.
We seek your joy, source of mirth and laughter,
for our limbs are weary and our hearts are heavy.
Set our minds on things that are excellent, admirable,
and worthy of praise.
Shine the light of your love far and wide,
that the world might strive after things
that are just, righteous, and true. Amen.

Words of Assurance (Philippians 4)
The peace of God, which passes all understanding,
is ours through Christ Jesus.
Rest secure in this assurance,
for it is trustworthy and true.

Passing the Peace of Christ (Philippians 4)
Keep your hearts and minds focused on things that are
excellent and admirable. God will surely bless you with
a peace that passes all understanding. Let us share signs
of this peace with one another.

Invitation to the Word (Philippians 4)
As we listen for the word of God, may our thoughts linger on what is honorable and true, just and pure, pleasing and commendable, excellent and worthy of praise.

Response to the Word (Philippians 4)
God's word invites us to bathe in the waters
of compassion and love.
Christ's example urges us to clothe ourselves
in justice and righteousness.
The Spirit's power inspires us to abide
in mercy and grace.

THANKSGIVING AND COMMUNION

Invitation to the Offering (Psalm 106)
> As recipients of God's steadfast love and grace, let us
> offer gifts of gratitude in our tithes and offering.

Offering Prayer (Psalm 106, Philippians 4)
> God of steadfast love, your bounty knows no bounds.
> For the abundant gifts in our lives,
>> we thank you.
> For the peace that passes all understanding,
>> we praise you.
> For keeping our hearts and minds in Christ Jesus,
>> we honor you.
> Receive the gifts we bring you this day,
>> and help us stay focused
>>> on things that are excellent and admirable,
>>>> holy and just, righteous and pure. Amen.

SENDING FORTH

Benediction (Philippians 4)
> May the peace of God,
>> which passes all understanding,
>> keep your hearts and minds in Christ Jesus,
>> from this day forward and forevermore. Amen.

October 22, 2023

Twenty-First Sunday after Pentecost
Proper 24

Mary Petrina Boyd

COLOR

Green

SCRIPTURE READINGS

Exodus 33:12-23; Psalm 99; 1 Thessalonians 1:1-10;
Matthew 22:15-22

THEME IDEAS

The holiness and goodness of God are found in all these
passages. Overwhelmed by the task ahead, Moses cries
out to God for guidance and presence. The Holy God
offers just a glimpse of the divine reality. The root of this
reality is goodness. Psalm 99 praises the holiness of God,
for God answers our cries with forgiveness and love. In
1 Thessalonians, Paul thanks the community (who live
by faith, hope, and love) as they serve the living God.
Jesus refuses to be drawn into arguments about taxes
but reminds us that our ultimate loyalty must be to God.

INVITATION AND GATHERING

Centering Words (Exodus 33)
> Seek God's presence, that God's goodness, mercy, and grace may bless and strengthen you. Who knows if the Lord may tuck you into a safe place and give you a glimpse of God's glory?

Call to Worship (Exodus 33)
> Come, Holy God, draw near.
> > **We long to see you.**
> Come, God of justice, be present today.
> > **We need your grace in our world.**
> Come in this hour.
> > **Show us your love.**

Opening Prayer (Exodus 33)
> Holy God, we long to sense your presence
> > and be assured that you have drawn near.
> Awaken us with your love and grace
> > and show us your possibilities for our lives.
> Assure us that we are not alone
> > and that you walk with us always.
> For this we offer you our thanks and praise. Amen.

PROCLAMATION AND RESPONSE

Prayer of Confession (Exodus 33, 1 Thessalonians 1)
> God of grace, though you are always present,
> > you often feel distant.
> Our minds seek to limit your reality
> > to things we can understand.
> Expand our imaginations,
> > that we may see your kindness and grace
> > > at work in the world around us.

When our work becomes a burden
and our struggles seem pointless,
save us from despair.
Remind us to ground ourselves in faith
and to reach out with hope and love,
as we seek to live in your ways. Amen.

Words of Assurance (Psalm 99)
When we cry out to you, O God, you answer us.
You receive us, forgive us, and show us your love.

Passing the Peace of Christ (1 Thessalonians 1)
Friends, you are God's beloved people, examples of
love and grace. Welcome one another with the love of
God and the peace of Christ.

Prayer of Preparation (Exodus 33)
God, you are wrapped in mystery
beyond human comprehension.
Open our hearts to your presence
as we seek your truth
within the words we are about to hear. Amen.

Response to the Word (Exodus 33)
Holy mystery, when we are overwhelmed by life,
tuck us in to a safe place
where we can see a glimpse of your goodness.
For you are vaster than anything we can imagine.
Amen.

THANKSGIVING AND COMMUNION

Invitation to the Offering (Matthew 22)
Jesus said, "Give to God, what belongs to God." We are
God's people, created in God's image. Everything we

are, and all that we have, comes from God. Out of gratitude for the abundance of God's gifts, let us bring our offering in gratitude and praise.

Offering Prayer (Exodus 33, 1 Thessalonians 1)
Holy God, your kindness and compassion surround us.
You alone are holy.
You alone bring meaning and hope to our lives.
We are grateful for all that you are
    and all that you give us.
Receive us and the gifts that we bring,
    that the world might know you
        and the gifts you offer to those who ask.
Amen.

SENDING FORTH

Benediction (Exodus 33, 1 Thessalonians 1)
Go from this place, persevering in faith, hope, and love.
May the goodness of God be with you.
May the love of God sustain you.
And may you go in peace.

October 29, 2023

Twenty-Second Sunday after Pentecost
Proper 25
Reformation Sunday

Kirsten Linford

Deut 6:4+5
Matt 22:34-40
645 O Master let me walk with Thee
591 Have Thine Own Way, Lord

COLOR

Green

SCRIPTURE READINGS

Deuteronomy 34:1-12; Psalm 90:1-6, 13-17;
1 Thessalonians 2:1-8; Matthew 22:34-46

THEME IDEAS

Though subtle, a common theme connects these lections. In its own way, each speaks to surprising or challenging experiences of answering God's call and doing God's work. In Deuteronomy, Moses arrives at the promised land, but cannot enter. He passes leadership to Joshua who will guide the people in. Psalm 90 speaks of God, who is the source of great power, with a longer vision than our own. Yet, the psalmist is bold enough to ask God to bless the people's labor—the work of their hands. (Is it God's work that has been placed in their hands?) Paul reminds the Thessalonians of his own calling—to share the gospel and even himself, despite opposition or maltreatment. And in Matthew, the authorized leaders ask Jesus to name the greatest commandment. Jesus responds with a charge to all the faithful: To love God with heart, soul, and mind; and to love one's neighbor as oneself.

INVITATION AND GATHERING

Centering Words (Psalm 90, Matthew 22)
Answer your greatest call: To love God with all that you are; and to love your neighbor as you love yourself. Do this and God will prosper the work of your hands.

Call to Worship (Psalm 90, Matthew 22)
God has been our dwelling place in all generations.
Before the mountains were brought forth,
before the earth and sky were formed,
God was from everlasting to everlasting.
We come to worship this day,
that God may gather us in.
We will be close to God's heart,
and we will dwell in God's grace.
We will love God fully,
and we will love one another well.

Opening Prayer (Psalm 90, Matthew 22)
God of Life, your memory is longer than time;
your love longer still.
Your giving nature amazes us.
You have given us yourself.
You have given us your work.
You only ask for love in return,
for you and for the world.
You put your ministry into our hands,
trusting us to be your hands.

Bless the work of our hands
    and the ministries of our hearts, O God,
        as we seek to do your will. Amen.

PROCLAMATION AND RESPONSE

Prayer of Confession (Psalm 90, 1 Thessalonians 2, Matthew 22)
    God of Mercy, we hear your command
        to love one another.
    These words are easy to say,
        yet so difficult to do.
    If only loving could be as natural as breathing,
        but it takes work and dedication.
    Even when we think we are following you, God,
        it is easy to get distracted, overwhelmed,
            turned around, even lost.
    We turn to the loud praise of the world,
        rather than the quiet whisper of your blessing.
    We do the simple, the least-resistant,
        and leave the difficult behind.
    Turn us around, God.
    Turn us back to you when we have wandered,
        when we have suffered,
            or when we bring suffering on others.
    Show us once more what love looks like
        and send us into the world
            to try again. Amen.

Words of Assurance (Psalm 90)
    When we lose our way;
        when we are confused and confounded,
        God waits with compassion, to turn us back
        to love, to grace, to God's own face.

Even before we ask for mercy,
    God has already forgiven us.
God sweeps away our mistakes and misdeeds
    and calls us home.

Passing the Peace of Christ (Psalm 90, Matthew 22)
    May the love of God, the peace of Christ, and the communion of the Holy Spirit be your dwelling place, now and forevermore. Amen.

Prayer of Preparation (Psalm 90)
    May the words of my mouth . . .
        and the meditations of our hearts
        be acceptable in your sight, O Lord,
        our strength and our redeemer. Amen.

Response to the Word (Deuteronomy 34, Psalm 90)
    Holy One, you have given us your word—
        both your scriptures and your promises.
    And you have kept them from generation to generation,
        in all times and places.
    Humbled and emboldened,
        we hear your call and vow to answer it.
    Make us your hands and feet,
        that we may love the world
        and so love you. Amen.

THANKSGIVING AND COMMUNION

Offering Prayer (Psalm 90, Matthew 22)
    Gracious God, you have given us mercy.
    You have given us love.
    You have been our calling,
        and you have been our home.

Take now our hands and feet, O God,
 and use them for your purposes.
Take now the offering
 of our hearts, minds, and souls.
Transform them into your love,
 your mercy, and your everlasting grace
 for all the world. Amen.

SENDING FORTH

Benediction (Matthew 22)
People of God, go forth into the world.
Love God.
Love your neighbors.
Love yourselves.
Go forth as people of love. Amen.

November 1, 2023

All Saints Day

B. J. Beu and Mary Scifres

COLOR

White

SCRIPTURE READINGS

Revelation 7:9-17; Psalm 34:1-10, 22; 1 John 3:1-3;
Matthew 5:1-12

THEME IDEAS

On this day, the people of God are challenged to be
the saints of God. Life's difficulties are not ignored or
downplayed in these scriptures, but comfort is assured
through the love and grace of God. God's power and
glory are honored, even as the sufferings of life are rec-
ognized. In these readings, we worship God and pray
for God's comfort. In these prayers, we find the hope
and the faith to become the saints of God.

INVITATION AND GATHERING

Centering Words (Revelation 7)
Blessing, honor, and glory to the Lord, our God. Praise
the ancient of days.

Call to Worship (Psalm 34)

Bless the Lord at all times.

Praise God's holy name.

Magnify the Lord with hearts full of devotion.

Sing of God's glory with tongues full of song.

Seek the Lord of love.

We will worship the living God.

Opening Prayer (Matthew 5)

Loving God, be with us in our time of worship.

Bless every enterprise of our lives,

that we might be a blessing to others.

Shower us with grace and mercy,

that we might bring grace and mercy

to a world in pain and want.

Give us pure hearts and humble spirits,

that we might show Christ's example

in all that we say and do.

Grant us hope and perseverance,

that we might live as saints,

as our foremothers and forefathers before us.

In faithful reverence, we pray. Amen.

–OR–

Opening Prayer (1 John 3, Matthew 5)

God of mercy and grace,

shower us with your loving kindness.

Fashion us into the saints you call us to be.

Love us abundantly,

that others may see your kindness and joy

reflected in our lives.

Bless us with your abiding presence,

that we may shine as saints of your holy love.

Amen.

PROCLAMATION AND RESPONSE

Prayer of Yearning (Matthew 5)
We yearn to be counted among the saints of old,
 but the journey is long and difficult.
We long to love others as we should,
 even when they revile and hate us.
We seek to forgive those who wrong us,
 even when it means swallowing our pride.
We strive for the openness of spirit
 to pray for those who persecute us,
  even when we want to hold onto our wounds.
Guide us on this journey of discipleship,
 that we may grow as your children
  and live as saints of your love. Amen.

Words of Assurance (1 John 3)
Beloved children of God, even when we fail,
 God's love never fails.
What we will be has not yet been revealed,
 but we know that we will be like Christ one day.
Until that day, trust that we are surrounded
 by the love and tender mercies of our God.

Passing the Peace of Christ (1 John 3)
The saints of God are all around us. With eyes ready to
see one another as we truly are, share signs of Christ's
peace this day.

Response to the Word (1 John 3)
We are loved by God.
 Thanks be to God.
Here and now, we are God's children.
 Praise be to our maker.

Love one another well.
**By this we will be known as Christ's disciples
and as saints of God.**
Thanks be to God!

THANKSGIVING AND COMMUNION

Offering Prayer (Matthew 5, Revelation 7)
Gracious one, you offer us the bread of life
and the living water of Christ.
We come before you to offer our hearts
and the riches we have received from your hand.
Bless these gifts,
that they may bring the Spirit's comfort
to those whose eyes are wet with tears.
In Christ's holy name we pray. Amen.

Invitation to Communion (Matthew 5, Revelation 7)
All who hunger for love,
come to the bread of life.
Here, all are fed.
All who thirst for the cup of blessing,
come to the table of grace.
Here, all are made whole.
All who need mercy and grace,
come to the Lamb of God.
Here, all find a home.

SENDING FORTH

Benediction (1 John 3)
Blessed are you, beloved children of God.
We will walk in the love given to us.
Be a blessing to all God's children.
**We will serve others with the grace
we have received.**
Walk in the footsteps of the saints of old.
**We will step gently upon the earth
and leave puddles of light for others to follow.**

November 5, 2023

Twenty-Third Sunday after Pentecost
Proper 26

B. J. Beu
Copyright © B. J. Beu

503 Since Jesus Came into My Heart

COLOR   *564 Just a Closer Walk w/ Thee*

Green

SCRIPTURE READINGS

Joshua 3:7-17; Psalm 107:1-7, 33-37;
1 Thessalonians 2:9-13; Matthew 23:1-12

THEME IDEAS

Jesus said, "The greatest among you will be your servant. All who exalt themselves will be humbled, and
all who humble themselves will be exalted" (Matthew
23:11-12 NRSV). These words capture today's theme. In
Joshua, the priests bearing the ark of the covenant must
risk looking foolish as they wade into the Jordan River
before the waters will part and the people are able to
walk across on dry ground. Jesus scolds the scribes and
the Pharisees for forsaking servant ministry in favor of
earthly recognition at social events. Paul reminds the
church at Thessalonica that those who brought them the

gospel worked day and night on their behalf so as not to be a burden on anyone. Humility and gratitude for God's blessings lead to servant ministry; they also bring a recognition of our dependence on God, one another, and the bounty of creation.

INVITATION AND GATHERING

Centering Words (Matthew 23)
The greatest must be the servants of all. So it is in God's upside down world—a world where the first shall be last and the last shall be first.

Call to Worship (Joshua 3, Matthew 23)
Called to service in Christ's name,
let us worship together and listen to God's word.
We gather to worship God
and bring comfort to those
who hunger and thirst.
Step confidently into the river of faith.
We gather to help one another
cross the River Jordan.
Come! Let us worship the Lord, our God.
We come to follow in the footsteps of Christ.

Opening Prayer (Psalm 107, Matthew 23)
Your steadfast love endures forever, O God.
How can we keep from singing your praises?
When we suffer from hunger and thirst,
    you deliver us from distress.
When our souls faint within us,
    you revive us with pools of clear water.
Help our hearts be humble,
        that we may seek the welfare of others
            before our own honor and glory.

In deepest humility,
    we ask that our steps never falter
        as we seek the welfare of all. Amen.

PROCLAMATION AND RESPONSE

Prayer of Yearning (Joshua 3, Psalm 107, Matthew 23)
    Strong deliverer, as we walk into the rivers of life,
        you part the waters and help us walk on dry ground.
    We yearn to feel worthy of your great love,
        but find it hard to humble ourselves
           and take the role of the servant.
    We long to release fears
        that we will lose power and prestige,
        that we will no longer hold places of honor,
        that we will be perceived as weak.
    Heal our insecurities, O God.
    Help us live Christ's truth
        that the greatest are those who serve,
           and that those who humble themselves
               will be exalted. Amen.

Words of Assurance (Matthew 23)
    Sisters and brothers in faith,
        Christ's grace saves us from our fears
        and leads us into a freedom the world cannot touch,
        much less take away.
    Rest in the assurance of God's redeeming love.

Passing the Peace of Christ (1 Thessalonians 2)
    As heirs with Christ, let us lead lives worthy of our calling by offering one another signs of love and peace.

Response to the Word (Joshua 3, Psalm 107, Matthew 23)
    Until the priests stepped in faith into the River Jordan,
    the waters cut off the people's safety on the other side.

Until we step into the waters of servant ministry,
God's words will not truly bear fruit in our lives.
Do not be hearers of the word only, but doers also.
We offer our humble service to the Lord of life.

THANKSGIVING AND COMMUNION

Invitation to the Offering (Psalm 107, Matthew 23)
The one who turns parched lands into springs of water, and feeds the hungry from fruitful fields, calls us to work for the healing of our world. As we collect this morning's offering, let us share generously from God's abundance.

Offering Prayer (Psalm 107)
Giver of all good things,
    we offer you our deepest gratitude.
We praise you for our many blessings:
    for water that refreshes,
    for fields that yield bountiful harvests,
    for wine that gladdens the heart.
May the gifts we bring this day
    go forth to bless your world with abundance,
        through Christ, our Lord. Amen.

SENDING FORTH

Benediction (Joshua 3, Matthew 23)
Step confidently into the waters of grace.
    God leads us into life.
Work humbly in the service of others.
    Christ leads us into life.
Proclaim boldly the glory of our God.
    The Spirit leads us into life.
Go with God's blessings.

November 12, 2023

Twenty-Fourth Sunday after Pentecost
Proper 27

Leigh Anne Taylor

642 Abide with me
43 All Hail the Power

COLOR

Green

SCRIPTURE READINGS

Joshua 24:1-3a, 14-25; Psalm 78:1-7;
1 Thessalonians 4:13-18; Matthew 25:1-13

THEME IDEAS

Listen for the arc of God's saving love throughout eternity
in today's readings. Joshua and the psalmist look deep
into our collective past "beyond the river" to our origin
with God. Matthew and Thessalonians cast an intoxi-
cating vision of intimacy with the Risen Christ and with
all who are, or have ever been, in a loving relationship
with him. Joshua and the psalmist remember the story of
God's saving love across millennia. Matthew, Joshua, and
the psalmist shake us awake to the present moment—
how shall we live right now? Will we find ourselves in
the story of God's love? Will we choose the rule of God's
love in the Risen Christ today and, thereby, receive hope
for the grief-filled now and a joy-filled eternity?

INVITATION AND GATHERING

Centering Words (Psalm 78, 1 Thessalonians 4)
Hope. Holy hope. Who guided you to God's rumbling
wellspring? Who needs you to point the way to God?

Call to Worship (Joshua 24, Psalm 78)
God is from everlasting to everlasting.
The Holy One inhabits all eternity
and everything that is, or was, or ever will be.
God is the source, guide, and goal of our lives.
We acknowledge God as the center of our lives
and of our world, not ourselves.
We come today to worship God.
We come with thanks and praise.
Let us humble ourselves before God's holy presence.
May God teach us the ways of life as we pray.

Opening Prayer (Matthew 25, 1 Thessalonians 4)
In the stillness of this moment,
awaken us to the astonishing truth
that your love is like the celebratory love
of a couple on their wedding day.
Help us choose again to live in your love
and to yield every aspect of our lives
to your divine rule. Amen.

PROCLAMATION AND RESPONSE

Prayer of Confession (Psalm 78, Matthew 25,
1 Thessalonians 4)
Christ Jesus, we want to believe in your kingdom—
a kingdom that is already, but not yet, in our midst.
It seems so far off as we bear our load
of suffering and grief.

Some days it's easier to get discouraged and distracted,
      even to give in to the long, dark nights
            of our worries and fears.
Sometimes it's easier to grow numb and lose hope,
      even to forget we even know you.
We want to trust that you haven't forgotten us.
We want to wake up and choose to live our lives
      inside the rule of your love.
We want to hope.
We want to offer wisdom and encouragement
      to the generations to come.
But we need your help.
In your mercy, hear our prayer. Amen.

Words of Assurance (Matthew 25)
Beloved of Christ, get up and get dressed,
      it is time to go to a wedding!
Trade your sweats for your fancy clothes.
Kick off your well-worn sneakers
      and lace up your dancing shoes!
Christ has already chosen you!
Will you choose to live in Christ's love?
      We choose God's saving love again.
      We choose holy joy for our lives.
      We choose the Risen Christ.
      Halleluia! Amen!

Introduction to the Word (Psalm 78)
Incline our ears to the words of your truth.
      In you, O God, we set our hope.

Response to the Word (Joshua 24, Psalm 78,
1 Thessalonians 4, Matthew 25)
Have you made your choice?
Are you prepared for the journey?

We will walk with God.
We will choose hope over despair.
Have you embraced your choice?
Are you ready to share the lessons you have learned?
We will live our choice.
We will teach our children
wisdom handed down of old.
(B. J. Beu)

THANKSGIVING AND COMMUNION

Offering Prayer (Joshua 24)
Holy God, we sometimes treat money as our god.
May we listen anew to Joshua's plea
that the Hebrew people put away foreign gods.
In our giving, free us from our love and worship
of money.
In today's offering, we choose to love again
and to worship you alone
in every aspect of our lives.
Receive our gifts with gratitude and praise
for your unending love. Amen.

SENDING FORTH

Benediction (Joshua 24, Psalm 78, Matthew 25,
1 Thessalonians 4)
Go with peace and with hope.
Find your place every day inside God's saving love.
Allow it to transform your ways.
Open your eyes to those who suffer
and offer God's love and hope
with lavish generosity.

November 19, 2023

Twenty-Fifth Sunday after Pentecost
Proper 28

Kirsten Linford

COLOR

Green

(handwritten: 539 May Faith Looks Up to Thee)
(handwritten: 597 Take My Life & Let it Be Consecrated)

SCRIPTURE READINGS

Judges 4:1-7; Psalm 123; 1 Thessalonians 5:1-11;
Matthew 25:14-30

THEME IDEAS

God's judgment and mercy do not always come as we expect them. Often, they arrive in surprising ways, at surprising times, and through surprising people. In Judges, God has sold the Israelites to King Jabin, only to hear their cry for help. God responds by sending deliverance through Deborah, the judge and prophet. Paul reminds the Thessalonians that God's judgment day will come unexpectedly like a thief in the night—except for those who keep awake and aware through faith, love, and the hope of salvation. And in Matthew, Jesus tells the parable of the talents, where those who risk the gifts they've been given are rewarded and the one who plays it safe is cast into outer darkness. Do these examples of

217

judgment and mercy continue to surprise us in our post-modern day and age?

INVITATION AND GATHERING

Centering Words (Psalm 123, 1 Thessalonians 5)
God's judgment comes in unexpected times and ways. Christ's mercy shows up through surprising people. When you are fed up and cry out for grace, keep awake, lest you fail to recognize it when it comes.

Call to Worship (Psalm 123, 1 Thessalonians 5)
We lift up our eyes to you, O God,
longing for a glimpse of your grace.
We watch for you . . . and wait,
trying to keep awake and aware,
trying not to fall asleep,
trying not to miss your presence,
trying not to miss our very lives.
Today, we come to you awake—
clothed in faith, decked out in love,
wearing hope for all to see.
Come and meet us here, O God,
in your mercy and your grace.

Opening Prayer (Psalm 123, 1 Thessalonians 5)
Holy One, have mercy on us.
When we cannot take any more of this world,
we know we must turn to you.
When our souls have had their fill
of trouble and unease,
we seek your protection.
We come to you in faith and love,
in the hope of your salvation,
now and always. Amen.

PROCLAMATION AND RESPONSE

Prayer of Confession (1 Thessalonians 5, Matthew 25)
We are not always awake, O God.
We are not always aware.
We do not always pay attention—
    to others,
    even to you.
We do not always treasure your blessings—
    the gifts you give to us,
    the time you spend with us,
    the people you offer us,
    the work you entrust to us.
We take it for granted, God.
We take *you* for granted.
We wander away.
Help us wake up, Holy One.
Remind us to be aware.
Show us the way back to you.
And help us find meaning in you once more.

Words of Assurance (1 Thessalonians 5, Judges 4)
The God of mercy hears our prayers
    and holds them close.
When we wander away into places of death and despair,
    God is always ready to bring us back.
For no matter where we go or what we do,
    we belong to God and God is there for us.
We belong to the one who clothes us in faith
    and hope and love.
We are held so close in God's hand
    that nothing can ever tear us away.

Passing the Peace of Christ (Psalm 123, 1 Thessalonians 5)
Children of God, see the Spirit's presence in yourselves
and in one another. May Christ's mercy be upon each
one of us, and may we all find Christ's peace this day.

Prayer of Preparation (Psalm 19)
May the words of my mouth . . .
and the meditations of our hearts
be acceptable in your sight, O Lord,
our strength and our redeemer. Amen.

Response to the Word (1 Thessalonians 5)
Grace upon Grace—
we are awakened by your mercy;
we are made wise by your word.
Fashion us into vessels fit to bear
the words of your mouth
and the meditations of your heart.
Speak through our very lives,
that we may be the voice of your hope
and your faith
and your everlasting love. Amen.

THANKSGIVING AND COMMUNION

Offering Prayer (1 Thessalonians 5)
Gracious God, you have filled our lives
with the protection of faith,
the guidance of love,
and the hope of a salvation without end.
Take our lives, Holy One—
our time, our talent, and our treasure—
and use them to encourage the hopeless,
to build up the broken,
and to heal the wounded souls
in our world. Amen.

SENDING FORTH

Benediction (1 Thessalonians 5)
> People of God—
>> put on hope, put on faith, and put on love.
> Go forth with hope to encourage one another.
> Go forth in faith to build each other up.
> Live in mercy . . . and abide in peace. Amen.

November 23, 2023

Thanksgiving Day

Michael Beu
Copyright © Michael Beu

COLOR

White

SCRIPTURE READINGS

Deuteronomy 8:7-18; Psalm 65; 2 Corinthians 9:6-15;
Luke 17:11-19

THEME IDEAS

The cycle of giving and gratitude flows through each
of today's Thanksgiving scriptures. These readings are
vivid reminders that giving, receiving, and thankfulness
are interrelated in both our spiritual and physical lives.
In giving, we are made more grateful for what we have
received. In giving thanks, we proclaim and honor the
giver and the gifts. Whether we are giving or receiving,
gratitude fuels this cycle and opens our hearts and lives
to receive the abundance of life more fully—the abundance promised and provided by the one who is giver
and maker of all.

INVITATION AND GATHERING

Centering Words (Psalm 65)
Overflow with beauty and joy like the pastures and hills of a verdant spring. Shout and sing praise like the meadows and valleys of an abundant harvest.

Call to Worship (Deuteronomy 8, Psalm 65, Luke 17)
Praise God, the giver of life.
Praise God, who blesses our world.
Praise God, who heals our wounds.
Praise God, who cares for our needs.
Praise God, the giver and maker of all.

Opening Prayer (Psalm 65, Luke 17)
Generous God of abundance and life,
thank you for the many gifts of our lives.
Thank you for this time of worship.
Thank you for your constant presence.
Thank you for your healing love.
Thank you, thank you, thank you.
In gratitude and joy, we pray. Amen.

PROCLAMATION AND RESPONSE

Prayer of Confession (Deuteronomy 8, Psalm 65, 2 Corinthians 9, Luke 17)
Creator of life and giver of all that we have,
thank you for your amazing grace
and your abundant love.
When we reject your many gifts,
forgive us.
Open our lives once more to your generosity.

When we neglect to give as generously
   as we have received,
      forgive our selfishness.
Draw us back to the generous love
   that first drew us into the mystery of your love
      and the marvels of your world.
When we forget to give thanks,
   forgive us.
Turn our thoughts back to you
   with joy and thanksgiving.
In your grace and love, we pray. Amen.

Words of Assurance (Psalm 65, Luke 17)
   Children of God, look up and give thanks
      for healing and forgiveness.
   Your faith has made you well.

*Response to the Word (Deuteronomy 8, Psalm 65,
2 Corinthians 9)*
   For food in our homes and roofs over our heads,
      we give God our thanks and praise.
   For healing in our bodies and renewal in our souls,
      we give God our thanks and praise.
   For gifts we can share and gifts we have received,
      we give God our thanks and praise.
   For this beautiful earth and its abundant provisions,
      we give God our thanks and praise.
   For friends and family and the kindness of strangers,
      we give God our thanks and praise.
   For Christ's call to live lives of purpose and passion,
      we give God our thanks and praise.

THANKSGIVING AND COMMUNION

Invitation to the Offering (2 Corinthians 9)
The one who sows sparingly will reap sparingly. The one who sows bountifully will reap bountifully. When we give with sincere, generous hearts, we sow a bounty of love and grace for those in need of our gifts. May each of us give as we will, not reluctantly, but with cheerful hearts and loving resolve.

Offering Prayer (2 Corinthians 9, Luke 17)
Generous, loving One, receive these gifts.
May they be symbols of your generous love
for all creation.
Bless these gifts and those who give them,
that all may become blessings to your world
and signs of your glory.
In your glory and grace, we pray. Amen.

SENDING FORTH

Benediction (2 Corinthians 9, Luke 17)
Get up and go on your way,
forgiven, healed, and free.
**We go to live what we have learned,
abundantly gifted and generously ready to give.**
Go to give and love freely.
**We go to serve God's world with generosity
and grace for all.**

November 26, 2023

Christh the King Sunday

Mary Scifres
Copyright © Mary Scifres

[handwritten: Lift High the Cross 450]

[handwritten: Come Thou Almighty King]

COLOR

White or Gold

SCRIPTURE READINGS

Ezekiel 34:11-16, 20-24; Psalm 100; Ephesians 1:15-23; Matthew 25:31-46

THEME IDEAS

These Christ the King readings invite us to become servants and to offer shepherding care to one another. Jesus lived this truth in his actions, but taught it powerfully in today's parable from Matthew 25. Power and dominion are not gilded with jewels and palaces. Rather, they carry great responsibility. To be the name above all names is to be the servant of all. To follow King Jesus is to follow a servant-leader; it is to serve with sacrificial love and empathetic compassion. What is the mark of a Christian follower? That we open our eyes, notice the needs of others, and respond with loving service to every member of God's creation, for all are sheep in the flock of God's world.

INVITATION AND GATHERING

Centering Words (Ephesians 1, Matthew 25)
Wisdom and truth touch our hearts and open our minds
when we open ourselves to Christ.

Call to Worship (Psalm 100, Matthew 25)
Make a joyful noise, a noise of service and love.
Praise God with lives of compassion.
Sing with acts of kindness.
Glorify God with acts of mercy.
Praise God with works of justice.
Praise God with overflowing love.

Opening Prayer (Ephesians 1, Matthew 25)
God of grace and God of glory,
reveal yourself through our lives and our love.
Shine your wisdom and truth into our hearts this day.
Help us know the hope to which we are called,
that we may be the servants you craft us to be.
In your glory and grace, we pray. Amen.

PROCLAMATION AND RESPONSE

Prayer of Yearning (Matthew 25)
Glorious God, shine the light of your love
in the lives of those who need it most.
May we see your glory reflected in them
and be reminded to shine your light
for all to see.
Speak to us through cries for help,
that we may hear and respond with compassion.
Reveal yourself in the lost and the lonely,
that we may be fully present to their needs.

For we yearn to notice you in our everyday living.
We long to set aside our fear and love courageously.
We hope with every fiber of our being
    to act as servants of your peace. Amen.

Words of Assurance (Ephesians 1)
    There is overwhelming greatness
        in God's power and grace.
    God's steadfast love lasts forever,
        offering grace upon grace
        and mercy upon mercy.

Response to the Word (Matthew 25)
    Compassionate God, help us show grace and mercy
        to everyone we meet.
    Help us see your face in every hungry child,
        in every tired woman,
            in every disappointed man.
    Help us hear your cry in every person who mourns,
        every person who is lonely,
            every person who groans in travail.
    Bathe us in your presence
        and grant us the courage and the confidence
            to act with compassion and love. Amen.

THANKSGIVING AND COMMUNION

Invitation to the Offering (Psalm 100, Matthew 25)
    With hearts wide open, with spirits ready to serve and
    give, let us bring our gifts and treasures to share with
    those in need of God's love.

Offering Prayer (Matthew 25)
    Shepherd of love, transform these gifts
        into nourishment for a hungry world.
    May they offer shelter from the storms of life.
    May they bring kindness and compassion
        to the lost and the lonely.
    Transform us, even as you transform these gifts,
        that we might be your hands and feet in the world.
    Amen.

SENDING FORTH

Benediction (Ezekiel 34, Matthew 25)
    Seek the lost and care for the wounded.
        We will strengthen the weak
        and encourage the downtrodden.
    Seek justice and love mercy.
        We will be God's mercy and love
        for the world.

[handwritten: Prophecy]

[handwritten: Hope]

December 3, 2023

First Sunday of Advent

B. J. Beu
Copyright © B. J. Beu

[handwritten: Matt 24:3b-44]

[handwritten: 245 O Come O Come]

COLOR *[handwritten: 526]* *[handwritten: Lift High the Solid Rock]*
Purple

SCRIPTURE READINGS

Isaiah 64:1-9; Psalm 80:1-7, 17-19; 1 Corinthians 1:3-9;
Mark 13:24-37

THEME IDEAS

Be not deceived, God is more than a loving parent who
dotes on beloved children; God is the awesome creator
whose presence makes the mountains quake. Isaiah
pleads for God to tear open the heavens and come down
to redeem Israel. For God hid from the people, and they
transgressed, only to face God's anger. The psalmist
calls on this angry God to restore and save us. God has
fed us with the bread of tears, but there is hope because
God is faithful. Mark's Gospel warns us to be awake, for
we know not when the master will return. Time is short,
so be ready; keep awake. The epistle reading does not
readily fit this theme but does proclaim that the hope
we look for is found in Christ, who strengthens us and
blesses us with spiritual gifts.

INVITATION AND GATHERING

Centering Words (Isaiah 64)
God is the potter; we are the clay. May God fashion us
into vessels of beauty and purpose this Advent season.

Call to Worship (Isaiah 64, Psalm 80)
The Lord of hosts redeems us when we stray.
With a mighty arm, God comes to save us.
When God hid his face, we strayed.
When God withdrew her presence, we stumbled.
God has fed us with the bread of tears
and given us tears to drink in full measure.
Yet, through his Son, God calls us back from the pit
and restores our future.
God shines upon us with love,
that we might be saved.
Come! Let us worship.

Opening Prayer (Isaiah 64, Mark 13)
God of glory, your power darkens the skies
and causes the moon to grow dim.
When we scatter to the four winds,
gather us from the ends of the earth
and restore us as your people.
Awaken us from slumber,
that we may be found ready
when the master of the house returns. Amen.

PROCLAMATION AND RESPONSE

Prayer of Yearning (Isaiah 64, Mark 13)
The mountains quake at your presence, O God.
The nations tremble at your feet.

Rather than rejoicing in our salvation,
    we have wandered from your path and lost our way.
Tear open the heavens and come down, Mighty One,
    as you did of old.
Awaken our world from slumber,
    and help your people stand in awe at your glory.
May your refiner's fire purify us of our transgressions,
    that we might be reshaped into vessels
        worthy of your kingdom. Amen.

Words of Assurance (Isaiah 64, 1 Corinthians 1)
We have been enriched in every way
    through the grace and peace of Christ.
When we abide in this grace and live in this peace,
    we are vessels worthy of God's kingdom.

Passing the Peace of Christ (1 Corinthians 1)
As heirs with Christ, let us lead lives worthy of our calling by offering signs of love and peace with one another.

Invitation to the Word (Isaiah 64)
O God, you are the potter; we are the clay.
As we listen for your word of life this day,
    fashion us into vessels fit for your purposes.
For we are your people, and you are our God.

Response to the Word or Benediction (1 Corinthians 1)
May the testimony of Christ be strengthened among us,
    that we may not lack any spiritual gift
    as we wait for the Lord.
May God strengthen us until the end,
    that we may be faithful in our fellowship with Christ
    and with one another.

THANKSGIVING AND COMMUNION

Offering Prayer (1 Corinthians 1)
    You have enriched us in every way, O God,
        through our faith in Christ Jesus.
    You have granted us grace
        and blessed us with every spiritual gift.
    In gratitude for your many blessings,
        we offer our tithes and offerings this day.
    Enrich and bless these gifts,
        that they may go into the world
            and help build your kingdom. Amen.

SENDING FORTH

Benediction (Mark 13)
    Keep awake; hope is coming to us.
    We await God's salvation.
    Keep alert; Christ is coming soon.
    We await God's blessings.
    Be ready; Christ is among us now.
    We go with God's blessing.

December 10, 2023

Second Sunday of Advent

Mary Scifres
Copyright © Mary Scifres

169 Rejoice ye Pure In Heart
705 It is well

COLOR

Purple

SCRIPTURE READINGS

Isaiah 40:1-11; Psalm 85:1-2, 8-13; 2 Peter 3:8-15a;
Mark 1:1-8

THEME IDEAS

Advent is a season of waiting, and today's scriptures convey this message vividly. God's promised world of righteousness awaits us, even as we await God's promised world. These scriptures also invite us to envision, and live into, the dream of a new heaven and a new earth. They invite us to imagine and even perceive a world where love and faithfulness meet, and peace and justice and righteousness dance together. John the Baptist calls us to prepare for this world. Such preparation requires forsaking any world where such things are missing. We are to live instead as people in whom love and faithfulness meet; and we are to dwell as a community of faith where peace, justice, and righteousness dance together.

INVITATION AND GATHERING

Centering Words (Psalm 85, 2 Peter 3)
In the waiting, God calls. May steadfast love and faithfulness rest in our souls. May justice, righteousness, and peace guide our steps and define our community of faith.

Call to Worship (Psalm 85, 2 Peter 3, Mark 1)
Prepare the path of God.
We prepare by waiting with patience.
Prepare the path of God.
We prepare by living with faith and love.
Prepare the path of God.
We prepare by pursuing justice and peace.
Prepare the path of God.
We prepare, we wait, we pray.
May God bless us with both patience and passion.
We wait and pray to create the path of God.

Opening Prayer (Psalm 85, 2 Peter 3, Mark 1)
While we are waiting, come to us, O God.
Reveal your presence in our time of worship.
Guide our steps in our speaking and our doing.
Flow through our lives, our church, and our world
with your steadfast love, unending faithfulness,
righteous justice, and mysterious peace.
In patient anticipation we pray. Amen.

PROCLAMATION AND RESPONSE

Prayer of Yearning (Psalm 85, 2 Peter 3, Mark 1)
Loving Shepherd, gather us in your arms of love.
Cover us with your mercy and grace,

that injustices might be healed
and transformed into righteousness,
justice and peace for your world.
Guide us to your path,
that we may be people who both await
and who create your path of peace, justice,
and love. Amen.

Words of Assurance (Isaiah 40, Psalm 85)
God will feed you with goodness and grace.
God will give you what is good—
mercy and forgiveness, love and acceptance,
an eternity of justice and peace.

Passing the Peace of Christ (Psalm 85)
May love and faithfulness meet as we gather together this day. May righteousness and peace define who we are as a community of faith. Share signs of this hope and promise as we greet one another this day.

Introduction to the Word (Psalm 85)
Hear what God will speak, for God speaks peace and salvation to those who listen.

Response to the Word (Psalm 85, 2 Peter 3, Mark 1)
While we wait, let us be God's people:
people of steadfast love.
While we wait, let us be God's people:
people of unending faithfulness.
While we wait, let us be God's people:
people of justice and righteousness.
While we wait, let us be God's people:
**people of peace who follow the Prince of Peace,
the one who is coming soon.**

THANKSGIVING AND COMMUNION

Offering Prayer (Isaiah 40, Psalm 85)
Shepherd of love, all you have given us is good:
love and justice, peace and righteousness,
faith and hope.
May the gifts we now give back to you
become gifts of love and justice,
peace and righteousness,
faith and hope. Amen.

Invitation to Communion (Isaiah 40, Psalm 85, 2 Peter 3)
The shepherd invites us to join the flock of God.
At the shepherd's table,
all are fed with love.
At the shepherd's table,
all are fed with grace.
At the shepherd's table,
all are welcome.
This is the table where steadfast love
and faithfulness meet.
This is the table where justice, righteousness,
and peace dance.
This is the table where the world is invited
to do the same.

SENDING FORTH

Benediction (2 Peter 3, Mark 1)
Go forth with patience to await Christ's arrival.
Go forth with passion to proclaim Christ's presence.
Go forth with perseverance to live Christ's promises.
Go forth to wait and create the path of God.

December 17, 2023

Third Sunday of Advent

B. J. Beu
Copyright © B. J. Beu

COLOR
Purple

SCRIPTURE READINGS
Isaiah 61:1-4, 8-11; Psalm 126; 1 Thessalonians 5:16-24; John 1:6-8, 19-28

THEME IDEAS

The one who restores Israel is the one who brings release to the captives, help to the oppressed, and joy to the brokenhearted. The one who restored Israel's fortunes in the time of Isaiah is the very one who sent John to make straight the way of the messiah. Now is the time to rejoice, to pray without ceasing, and to prepare for our salvation.

INVITATION AND GATHERING

Centering Words (Isaiah 61)
God's faithful live as oaks of righteousness. Let us grow strong and true this Advent season.

Call to Worship (Psalm 126, Isaiah 61)
When the Lord restores our fortunes,
we are like those who dream.
Our mouths are filled with laughter;
our hearts sing with shouts of joy.
Worship the Lord of our salvation.
Worship the Lord!

Opening Prayer (Psalm 126, Isaiah 61)
God of Dreams, you have done great things
for your people.
From times of old, you awaken the faithful
to the dawn of your glory.
Fill our mouths with laughter.
Loose our tongues with shouts of joy.
Anoint us with the oil of gladness
and make it known among all people
that we will live as oaks of righteousness,
the plantings of the Lord. Amen.

PROCLAMATION AND RESPONSE

Prayer of Yearning (Isaiah 61, John 1:23 NRSV)
Merciful God, we hear John's fervent cry:
"Make straight the way of the Lord,"
but we don't know what we should do.
Our lives carry on as they have before.
Nothing seems to change.
Yet we long to be caught up in the ecstatic visions
of prophets and mystics.
We yearn to tune our ears to the heralds
who testify to your light.
Help us walk in the ways that lead to life,
through Jesus Christ, our Lord. Amen.

Words of Assurance (1 Thessalonians 5)
> The God of peace sanctifies us,
>> that our souls may be sound and blameless.
> The one who calls is faithful.
> The one who saves fashions us for eternal life.

Passing the Peace of Christ (Isaiah 61)
> Clothed in the garments of salvation and the robes of righteousness, let us celebrate God's love by sharing the peace of Christ.

Response to the Word (1 Thessalonians 5:18-19)
> Rejoice always.
> Pray without ceasing.
> Give thanks in all circumstances,
>> for this is God's will in Christ Jesus.
> Let your prayers be made known to God,
>> and do not quench the Spirit,
>>> for such is the honor due to our God.

THANKSGIVING AND COMMUNION

Offering Prayer (Isaiah 61, Psalm 126, 1 Thessalonians 5)
> God of peace, you have restored our hope
>> and sanctified our dreams.
> May this offering express the joy we feel
>> for the gift of your salvation.
> May our gifts reflect our wonder and gratitude
>> for being clothed in the garments of salvation
>>> and the robes of righteousness.
> May our tithes and our very lives
>> help restore the dreams of the downhearted,
>>> and fill the hungry with good things. Amen.

SENDING FORTH

Benediction (Isaiah 61, Psalm 126, 1 Thessalonians 5)
Go forth, sanctified in the love of God.
God has turned our weeping into laughter.
Go forth, clothed in the garments of salvation
and the robes of righteousness.
Christ has turned our sorrow into joy.
Go with God.

Love — Ang!

December 24, 2023

Fourth Sunday of Advent

B. J. Beu
Copyright © B. J. Beu

104 O Worship the King
250 O Little Town

COLOR

Purple

SCRIPTURE READINGS

2 Samuel 7:1-11, 16; Luke 1:46-55; Romans 16:25-27; Luke 1:26-38

THEME IDEAS

Glory is owed to our God. David wishes to build God a house but is told that God does not need a temple to be glorified. Mary's Magnificat glorifies God for lifting up the lowly, casting down the proud, and filling the hungry with good things. And Mary and Elizabeth carry children that will glorify God in the lives they lead. Truly, glory is owed to our God.

INVITATION AND GATHERING

Centering Words (Luke 1, Romans 16)

Glorify God this day. Magnify the Lord with all your heart. Sing praises to God who reigns above. Glorify the Lord with gladness.

Call to Worship (Luke 1, Romans 16)
Relatives conceive—one a barren woman,
the other a young girl who has not been with a man.
How can this be?
With God, all things are possible.
Our hearts beat with laughter.
Our lips sing of God's glory.
Let us magnify the Lord as we worship God this day.

Opening Prayer (Luke 1, Romans 16)
Come to us, Promised One,
in this season of waiting.
Set our hearts ablaze with the glory of your salvation.
Set our minds afire with the richness of your word.
Reveal to us the secret of your ways;
for you alone are wise,
you alone are worthy of our thanks and praise.
Through Jesus Christ, our Lord, we pray. Amen.

PROCLAMATION AND RESPONSE

Prayer of Yearning (Luke 1, Romans 16)
God of grace and God of glory,
pour your power on your people.
We long for the strength and the courage
to glorify your name in all that we say
and in all that we do.
Open our eyes to the promise of your salvation,
as you scatter the proud,
pull down the powerful from their thrones,
fill the hungry with good things,
and send the rich away empty.
Live in and through us this Christmas season,
that we might be messengers of your grace
and instruments of your peace. Amen.

Words of Assurance (Luke 1, Romans 16)
> The secret that was kept quiet for so long
>> has been revealed in Christ.
> All are loved and all will be saved
>> by the searching love of our Lord and savior.

Passing the Peace of Christ (Luke 1)
> As was promised to our ancestors, God has come to live with us and redeem us. In joy and deepest gratitude, let us turn to one another and share signs of the peace we find in Christ.

Response to the Word (Luke 1)
> Magnify the Lord with hearts full of love.
> **Sing to the Lord with souls full of joy.**
> For the Mighty One has done great things for us.
> **Holy is God's name.**
> Surely goodness and mercy will follow us
> all the days of our lives.
> **And we will dwell in the house of the Lord forever.**

THANKSGIVING AND COMMUNION

Offering Prayer (Luke 1)
> Loving God, your goodness and mercy
>> are without limit.
> With thankful hearts,
>> we bring our offering before you this day.
> Use these gifts to lift up the lowly,
>> fill the hungry with good things,
>>> and bring hope to all who call on your name.
> In Jesus's name, we pray. Amen.

SENDING FORTH

Benediction (Luke 1, Romans 16)
Go forth, glorifying God with hearts full of joy.
Praise God with lips filled with laughter.
Bless the world with the mercy and grace
you have received from God's hand.
Go in the fullness of God's blessings.

December 24, 2023

Christmas Eve

Mary Petrina Boyd

COLOR

White

SCRIPTURE READINGS

Isaiah 9:2-7; Psalm 96; Titus 2:11-14; Luke 2:1-20

THEME IDEAS

We gather to hear the familiar story of the birth of Jesus. We bring great longing: longing for a deep encounter with the sacred, longing for a sense of peace, longing for a reason to hope. More than a cozy story of a baby born in a stable, this night tells us that the realm of justice and peace has broken into our world. In this infant, we see one of great strength and power who brings salvation and joy to the world.

INVITATION AND GATHERING

Centering Words (Isaiah 9)

This is a night of deep joy. A child is born for us, a child who brings peace.

–OR–

Centering Words (Luke 2)

On this holy night, we meet a great mystery. In the quiet of a stable, we hear the cry of a newborn child. In the stillness of a field, we see the glory of God. Come and find the mystery of love.

Call to Worship (Luke 2)

The night was dark.
A baby lay in a manger.
The night was still.
Angels sang to shepherds.
The night was expectant.
God's glory shone brightly.
On this night,
let us rejoice in the gift of love.

–OR–

Call to Worship (Luke 2)

What's happening?
A child is born.
Who is this child?
This is Jesus, God's gift to us.
Let's go see!
The baby is in a manger.
Let's go tell!
Jesus is born!
Let's praise God!
Glory to God!

–OR–

Call to Worship (Psalm 96)

Let the heavens celebrate!
Let the earth rejoice!

Let the seas roar with praise!
Let the trees shout with joy!
Jesus is born!
**Glory to God in the highest heavens
and peace to all on earth!**

Opening Prayer (Luke 2)
Loving God, this is a holy night.
We come longing to hear your story
of new life and hope.
Speak your words of truth and power.
May the gift of your love
be born anew among us.
Cast out our fears,
that we may rejoice in your power
and your goodness. Amen.

–OR–

Opening Prayer (Luke 2)
Holy One, open our hearts
to receive the true gift of Christmas.
May the stillness of your peace wash over us.
May we encounter hope born anew.
We are here, waiting for you,
ready to receive your gift of love.
Be with us now,
as we come and adore the newborn child.
Amen.

PROCLAMATION AND RESPONSE

Prayer of Yearning (Isaiah 9)
We often come to Christmas
longing for a cozy story
of a baby born in a manger.

But this baby will change the world.
He is called Wonderful Counselor, Mighty God,
    Prince of Peace.
Something strong and powerful began with that infant.
He brings justice and righteousness for all the world.
Enlarge our minds, increase our vision,
    and strengthen our commitment,
        that we too may work for justice
        and righteousness.
Help us walk faithfully with him,
    and lead us on your paths of peace. Amen.

Words of Assurance (Titus 2)
Jesus is our blessed hope,
    bringing grace and salvation to all.
On this night of nights,
    we are loved and made whole.

–OR–

Words of Assurance (Isaiah 9)
Jesus is the child born for us.
He is the Wonderful Counselor, Mighty God,
    Eternal Parent, Prince of Peace.
Rejoice in this good news!

Passing the Peace of Christ (Luke 2:14)
The angels sang to shepherds: "Glory to God in the
highest heavens and peace to God's people on earth."
Greet one another with this heaven-sent peace.

Prayer of Preparation (Luke 2)
God of love, open our hearts
    to hear this familiar story with new hope.
Speak your wisdom of love and peace.
Let your grace flow over us,
    as new life is born. Amen.

Response to the Word (Luke 2)
> Holy God, you entered our world as a vulnerable infant,
>> bringing hope and peace to all creation.
> Your hope transforms our despair.
> Your peace fills us with deep joy.
> Your presence destroys our fears.
> As Mary treasured the words she heard,
>> so may we treasure this story.
> As the shepherds praised God,
>> so may we praise your amazing love. Amen.

THANKSGIVING AND COMMUNION

Invitation to the Offering (Luke 2)
> On this night, we remember God's gift of Jesus. Having heard the song of the angels, the shepherds had to see for themselves. They returned praising God for this amazing gift. May our gifts today echo their praise. Thank you, God, for Jesus.

Offering Prayer (Luke 2)
> Holy God, we are grateful for the incredible gift
>> born in a stable in Bethlehem.
> The love and joy birthed by Jesus
>> has touched and transformed our lives.
> We bring our gifts to you this night.
> We bring our gifts of money
>> to continue your mission of peace.
> We bring our hearts,
>> as we adore you and long to follow Jesus. Amen.

SENDING FORTH

Benediction (Luke 2)

    We have heard the Christmas story of love—
        love born in a manger.
    Like the shepherds,
        we found the Christ child.
    Like Mary,
        we hold this story deep in our hearts.
    Let us join the angels,
        telling this news of incredible joy.
    And may God's blessing of peace
        be ours this night and forevermore.

–OR–

Benediction (Luke 2)

    Listen! Do you hear the angels singing?
        "Glory to God in highest heaven
        and on earth, peace to all"?
    This peace is yours for the asking,
        a gift from God this night.
    Go in peace.

December 31, 2023

First Sunday after Christmas Day

Catarina Paton

COLOR

White

[handwritten: 196 O Come, Let Us Adore Him]
[handwritten: 281 What Child is This]

SCRIPTURE READINGS

Isaiah 61:10–62:3, Psalm 148, Galatians 4:4-7, Luke 2:22-40

[handwritten: 2:22 - 33; 39-40]

THEME IDEAS

The glory of God's salvation through Christ is juxta-posed with the ritual presentation of a young Jewish boy at the temple. Even as his family participates in this common custom, the uncommon breaks in. Sime-on proclaims Jesus to be the long-awaited Messiah, the salvation for which Simeon has waited. Anna praises God for this young child, in whom she sees "the re-demption of Jerusalem" (Luke 2:38). Christmas is a reminder that our extraordinary God breaks into our ordinary world, our ordinary lives, and our ordinary traditions.

(B. J. Beu)

INVITATION AND GATHERING

Centering Words (Isaiah 61–62)

How can you stay silent in the joy of the Messiah's birth? Rejoice and sing God's praises, for the Lord's glory is with you this day.

Call to Worship (Psalm 148)

With mighty mountains and crashing seas,
praise the name of the Lord.
With rolling valleys and lush forests,
praise the name of our God.
With tiny ants and majestic eagles,
praise the name of the Holy One.
With innocent children and wise elders,
praise the name of Love.

Opening Prayer (Isaiah 61–62)

Almighty creator, we come to shout and rejoice
in the wonderful gift of your Son for our world.
It is a miracle that fills our lives with your glory.
On this last day of the year, may our celebration
honor the good we have received from your hand,
even as we look forward
to walking faithfully with you
in the year ahead.
As those who came before us,
we will not be silent in our love for you;
we will not mute our pure joy
for what you have brought to our lives. Amen.

PROCLAMATION AND RESPONSE

Prayer of Yearning (Isaiah 61–62, Luke 2)
We come to you with joy and happiness,
    but we know it won't always be so.
The human heart is a fickle thing.
As we celebrate the birth of your Son,
    open us to the many ways you seek to bless us.
Free our lips to sing your praises,
    even when we feel alone and in need.
As a new year dawns,
    help us bring righteousness and praise
        to all the earth in your heavenly name. Amen.

Words of Assurance (Luke 2, Galatians 4, Psalm 148)
Through praise and thanksgiving,
    glory is given to God's name.
Guided by the Holy Spirit,
    see what God's salvation has brought
    to God's precious children.

Passing the Peace of Christ (Psalm 148)
In this time of glory and praise, let us rejoice by sharing
signs of Christ's peace.

Response to the Word (Luke 2, Galatians 4, Psalm 148)
Just as you have brought your child into this world,
    so you have brought us to be your children.
You have gifted us with your wisdom and glory,
    trusting that we will lead our lives in your name.
Praise the Lord. Amen.

THANKSGIVING AND COMMUNION

Offering Prayer (Psalm 148, Luke 2)
God of the heavens and the earth,
we come before you in celebration,
bringing gifts for those who cannot celebrate
with us.
Our songs of praise are for your name and honor.
May these gifts give others the opportunity
to sing praises to your name
as they come to know the endless love
you have for each of your children. Amen.

SENDING FORTH

Benediction (Galatians 4)
Go. Be a bright light and example to the world.
Show everyone you meet what it means
to be a child of God.
Help them see themselves as God sees them.

Contributors

B. J. Beu is a pastor, spiritual director, and coach who has served churches in the United Church of Christ for more than 30 years, most recently as Senior Pastor of Manhattan Beach Community Church in California.

Michael Beu is lead technology coordinator at United Methodist Church of Vista in Vista, California, while also serving as filmmaker and editor for a dance company, several churches, and two colleges. He has a film-editing degree in Cinema and Television Arts from California State University, Northridge. Find out more at: http://element productions.net/.

Mary Petrina Boyd is pastor of Langley United Methodist Church on Whidbey Island, Washington. She spends alternating summers working as an archaeologist in Jordan.

Joanne Carlson Brown is a retired United Methodist minister and professor of United Methodist theology at Seattle U School of Theology and Ministry in Seattle, Washington.

James Dollins is senior pastor of Anaheim United Methodist Church in Southern California, where he lives with his wife, Serena, and sons, Forrest and Silas. He is a lover of music, intercultural ministries, and God's creation.

Karin Ellis is senior pastor of La Cañada United Methodist in southern California. She enjoys parenting her two children with husband John and writing children's stories and liturgy for worship.

Paula A. Ferris is senior pastor of Fullerton First United Methodist Church in Fullerton, California.

Rebecca J. Kruger Gaudino, a United Church of Christ minister, teaches biblical studies and theology at the University of Portland (Oregon) and also writes for the church.

Amy B. Hunter is a poet and writer. She serves as lay associate for spiritual formation at All Saints Episcopal Church in Chelmsford, Massachusetts, and she has contributed to such publications as Religion Online and The Christian Century.

Sara Lambert is wife, mom, nurse, child of God, and has served as worship coordinator in The United Methodist Church.

Kirsten Linford grew up in Red Rock Christian Church in Boise, Idaho, and has strong Disciples roots. She is currently the pastor of Westwood Hills Congregational Church (UCC) in Los Angeles. Active in both the Disciples and UCC churches, she has served on committees at both the association/conference and national levels. Kirsten shares her life with her young daughter, Riley, and their golden retriever, Seamus.

Catarina Paton studied music and worship at Azusa Pacific University. She works in worship production at churches in southern California, but remains a member of Laguna Beach United Methodist Church.

Silvia Purdie is a minister in the Presbyterian Church of Aotearoa New Zealand, with a background in youth and children's ministry and counseling.

Mary Scifres is a United Methodist pastor, motivational speaker, teacher, and author who brings both inspiration and expertise for twenty-first-century leadership in creative worship, church growth, change management, visioning, and strategic planning. Learn more at www.maryscifres.com.

Leigh Ann Shaw is the senior pastor at United Methodist Church of Vista in Vista, California.

Leigh Ann Taylor is a Deacon in the Virginia Conference of the United Methodist Church, serving as Revitalization Coordinator for the Lynchburg District after three decades in full-time music ministry in Texas, Kansas, and Virginia. She also serves as president of The Fellowship of United Methodists in Music and Worship Arts.

Look for These New Titles
from Abingdon Press

Scripture Index

Old Testament

Genesis

Exodus

Deuteronomy

Joshua

Judges

1 Samuel

2 Samuel

Psalms

261

New Testament

Made in United States
Orlando, FL
06 November 2022